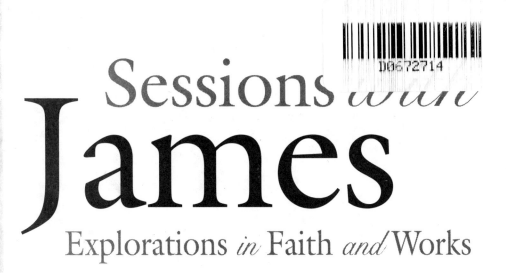

Sessions *with*
James

Explorations *in* Faith *and* Works

Michael D. McCullar

SMYTH&HELWYS
PUBLISHING, INCORPORATED • MACON, GEORGIA

Smyth & Helwys Publishing, Inc.
6316 Peake Road
Macon, Georgia 31210-3960
1-800-747-3016
© 2001 by Smyth & Helwys Publishing
All rights reserved.
Printed in the United States of America.

The paper used in this publication meets the minimum
requirements of American National Standard for Information
Sciences—Permanence of Paper for Printed Library Materials.

Library of Congress Cataloging-in-Publication Data

McCullar, Michael D.
Sessions with James / Michael D. McCullar.
p. cm.
Includes bibliographical references.
(pbk.)
1. Bible. N.T. James—Textbooks.
I. Title.
BS2785.55 .M33 2001
227'.9107—dc21

2001020305

ISBN 1-57312-358-7

Table of Contents

Sessions with James v

Introducing James vii

Session 1
Is This a Multiple-Choice Test? 1

Session 2
Is My Wisdom Showing? 9

Session 3
If I Were a Rich Man... 17

Session 4
Temptation Stands on Every Corner and Calls My Name 25

Session 5
You Have Two Ears but Only One Mouth...Ever Wonder Why? . . .33

Session 6
Playing Favorites with Favorites 41

Session 7
Baptized Nouns or Baptized Verbs? 51

Session 8
Wise as a Three-Dollar Bill 59

Session 9
In This Corner... 69

Session 10
How's the Ol' Future View? 79

Session 11
Excuse Me, Sir, Have You Seen My Heart? 87

Bibliography 93

Sessions with James

Sessions with James is an eleven-session study unit designed to give the learner a full understanding of the book of James.

James is a book filled with wisdom and practical knowledge that can assist believers in dealing with the Xs and Os of daily life. It is more ethics-centered than classic theology-centered, which allows for its ready practicality. James can be a tool for today's believer to utilize for lifestyle faith. Plus, James is about faith as well. Contrary to the earlier critics who stated that James was all about works, the book deals with what genuine faith produces and creates. This makes James a quite conclusive work.

Resource Pages

Each session is followed with resource pages consisting of 8-10 questions. Use the resource pages to allow for a deeper experience in the book of James. The resource pages may be used by a seminar leader during preparation and planning. The pages may also be used for individual study.

Introducing James

The book of James is the Rodney Dangerfield of the New Testament. There has been much derision of the text and many attempts to exclude it from canonized Scripture. In 1522, Martin Luther went as far as to refer to James as "a rather straw-like epistle" (Peace, Coleman, Sloan, Tardif, 9). James was thought to be too deeds-oriented when held up against the writings of Paul, who majored on justification by faith. It was also said to mention too little of Christ's suffering, crucifixion, and resurrection. There is no mention of the Holy Spirit and only two references to the name of Christ. When examples are given, only Old Testament prophets are named. Obviously this is not average to the New Testament.

James seems to stand out in the New Testament as Proverbs or Ruth does in the Old Testament. Being different does not make it less necessary nor does it preclude its "faith-weight." Herder wrote, "If the epistle is of straw, then it contains a very hearty, firm, nourishing...grain" (Peace, Coleman, Sloan, Tardif, 9).

James is a book filled with wisdom and practical knowledge that can assist believers in dealing with the Xs and Os of daily life. It is more ethics-centered than classic theology-centered, which allows for its ready practicality. James can be a tool for today's believer to utilize for lifestyle faith. James is about faith as well. Contrary to the earlier critics who stated that James was all about works, the book deals with what genuine faith produces and creates. This makes James a quite conclusive work.

Date

There is debate concerning the date of authorship of James. J. B. Major, a scholar of the early twentieth century, regarded James as the earliest work in the New Testament. Major, along with many conservative scholars, believed James to have been written between A.D. 40 and A.D. 50. Others date the book in the early 60s, citing the implied knowledge of Paul's work through chapter two. (Paul did not come upon the scene until the 50s.) It is a certainty that James, the brother of Jesus, was put to death due to Jewish hostility in A.D. 62. Some suggest that if James were indeed the author, that someone may have contributed to the work after his death.

Authorship

Of the author, verse 1 simply says, "James, a servant of God and of the Lord Jesus Christ" (NKJV). Since there are four individuals named James mentioned in the New Testament, there is much debate over which one authored the book. Two of the four mentioned were apostles—James the son of Zebedee and brother of John, and James the son of Alphaeus. The writer does not identify himself as an apostle. This makes it both easier and more difficult to assign authorship. James the son of Zebedee was martyred no later than A.D. 44. James the son of Alphaeus is seen as a lightweight as defined by activity and influence. Another James is mentioned but once and has never been seen as a candidate for authorship. The fourth James, oldest of the four brothers of Jesus, is widely regarded as the author of this work.

This in and of itself is amazing. James was not thought to be close to his brother Jesus. There are indications in Mark 3 and Luke 4 that his brothers were involved in his hometown's thinking that Jesus was quite mad. At the cross, Mary was present, but none of his brothers were.

However, things changed one day after the resurrection. First Corinthians 15:7 records that Jesus appeared to his brother and conversion followed. James the brother of Jesus went on to become the leader/pastor of the church in Jerusalem. He is also regarded as a man of great piety who had extraordinary faith development practices.

Audience

James is one of seven books in the New Testament known as general epistles, letters with no single, specific destination. What makes James different is the broad description of its intended readers: "To the twelve tribes scattered abroad." Is he writing to only Jewish Christians who were scattered around the known world due to persecution? Peter uses a similar phrase in his first letter, but his is blatantly directed to Gentile believers. They were often referred to as the *New Israel*.

Again, debate has raged for years on this issue. Many believe that the intended audience was exclusively Jewish Christians. This belief is substantiated by the fact that James was the spiritual leader of the Jerusalem church, a church primarily comprised of Hebrew believers. Others site the fact that in Christ Jesus there are no longer any former distinctions and that any and all believers make up the true *New Israel*. It is quite safe and sound to read this work with a universal approach. The truths that flow from this work are applicable for all believers who call upon the name of Christ, this being true both then and now.

Purpose

There is no doubt that James is one of the most practical books in all of Scripture. It majors on an active faith. It is very deliberate in its directive content, with the lessons following that direction in a somewhat repetitive thematic style. The repetitive nature simply underscores the major elements that are being stressed. James is successful in providing a "faith with works" framework that can complement and complete a firm New Testament theology. Practical instruction for practical living is another way to adequately characterize the work. James provides insight into the failures and pitfalls of Christian living. Fortunately, he also provides insight into the victories available to those who faith Christ with genuine devotion. It is a book of points (both positive and negative) and lessons for sinners. With that in mind, the purpose will be remarkably clear after reading the book of James.

1 Is This a Multiple-Choice Test?

Session   *James 1:2-4*

Have you ever wondered what it would feel like to be stranded in a foreign land basically alone? Different culture...different language...different people.

The letter James wrote was destined for people just like that. A New Testament era dispersion was in effect, and believers were scattered across the known world. Persecution by government officials and by rabid Orthodox Jews would soon force the church in Jerusalem to fold and hundreds of new converts to flee to places unknown to them.

This letter was intended for people living this type of exiled existence. The Christian movement was still very young. Churches were formative and had been established just long enough to be targets. Rome was regularly quelling rebellions and easily saw the new Christian church as both nuisance and threat. The Jews were angry, organized, and had a death wish for the perceived schism. As mentioned earlier, the largest and most influential church would crash due to persecution a few years after this letter was written. It was not uncommon for new believers to lose their livelihoods, as well as their homes, and become estranged from their families because of their faith in Jesus Christ. A unique New Testament *Catch-22* existed: with no hope of plying their trades and no place to live, most had to move on. This quandary, along with widespread dispersion at the hands of Rome and the Jewish forces, led most believers to scatter. As with the words of Jesus, *Foxes have holes and birds of the air have nests, but the Son of Man has nowhere to lay His head* (Matthew 8:20 [NKJV]), these first-century Christians no longer had a place to call home.

To have a faith life was tough in the first century. At its easiest, it was uncomfortable...at its hardest, deadly. Yet the vast majority of these new believers kept their faith. How? Refer back to the earlier question about being stranded in a foreign land. In that situation, what would benefit you the most? A guide? A hope for a better future? A how-to-survive manual?

This letter became all of these and more for the first-century believers who were living a scattered, scared, and confused life. It provided a guide for living the faith commitment in these new regions, among different people. It provided hope, order and structure amidst raging chaos. It defined the abiding grace of God to his faithful followers.

Good thing, because straightaway James deals with the biggest issue facing these new followers of Christ:

> My Brethren, count it all joy when you fall into various trials, knowing that the testing of your faith produces patience. But let patience have its perfect work, that you may be perfect and complete, lacking nothing. (1:2-4 [NKJV])

What do you think of when you hear the words *trials in life?* Most likely it's the same response as when the word *suffering* is uttered—negative, negative, negative. Trials are not usually thought of as positive. Does the term *joy* usually come to mind when contemplating *suffering* or *trials?* Not likely. Yet James is telling his readers that they must face the trials of life with joy! No wiggle room allowed. They aren't even allowed to moan a little.... *O Woest Me!*

Actually it's even more challenging after a word study is undertaken. "In the Greek text, the word translated as pure is the word *pas*, which is a primary word meaning all, every, and whole or thoroughly" (Cedar, 20). The conundrum grows!

Let's begin with a definition of *trial.* Webster defines trial as, "subjection to suffering or grief; tribulation; distress." James uses the Greek word *peirasmos*, which conveys an external testing of sorts. This same Greek word, *peirasmos*, is also used to describe temptation. In Matthew 6:13, Jesus uses the word to describe temptation in the prayer he taught his disciples. The writer of Hebrews uses the word to describe both trials and temptations faced by the Israelites (Hebrews 3:8).

So *trial* has multiple connotations as used in the New Testament. *Trial* can be used to describe an outward testing, garden variety temptation, and, by using the directional writing of James, persecution due to one's faith. This multiple definition of *trial* was standard operating procedure for James. With this in mind, it's easier to gauge the difficulty factor in following his command to "count it all joy!" No matter the circumstance or scope of the dilemma, "count it all (complete, thorough, total) joy!"

If you are persecuted for your faith, even to the death, respond with total joy.
If a natural disaster destroys all you possess, count it all joy.
If Satan hounds you relentlessly with temptation after temptation, move forward with the countenance of absolute joy.

The question that begs to be asked is *how?*

How does one respond with complete joy to brutal hostility brought about by one's faith?

How can a person be filled with joy while being tempted by Satan, especially if temptation wins?

Is it possible to live in a state of joy while at the same time picking up the pieces of one's former existence?

It would seem that any of the aforementioned negative possibilities could lead to either negative feelings toward God, negative feelings about one's self, or total resignation. Not one of these possible end results is remotely positive. Huge numbers of people have turned on God after a bad event marred their lives.

How could God allow a small child to die?
If God is in control, why did he allow a tornado to destroy so many lives?
If God is love, why does he allow so much suffering?

Strangely, even people in the process of spiritual anger and resignation use the word "allow." While some obviously and blatantly blame God and use terms that assign total fault, most seem to see God as "allowing" or "permitting" events to unfold. One approach borders on condemnation and assigns God to heartless despot status. The other recognizes God's omnipotence, but questions why things happen the way they do. The former conveys precious little hope. The latter can be the early steps on a spiritual journey of enlightenment.

These steps are crucially important. This journey is one that all believers must accept and begin. This is truly a journey of faith that requires an open mind, a thinking mind. Too many believers demand a concrete handle on things that are greatly abstract. There is absolutely no way to figure out everything in life. No doubt millions of people have tried, and all have failed. Deem them the mysteries of God. Say that life is bumpy and rough. Quote M. Scott Peck as he summed up life as being difficult. Any way one cuts it, life can be nasty at times. Our biggest quest is not to "figure it out," but how to accept and deal with these inevitable calamities. And this all-important quest often begins with our theology of God.

Determine Our Theology Regarding God's Will

One way to quickly end all debate over suffering and pain is to assign all blame to God's will. *Someone dies in a car crash...God's will. A sudden cardiac arrest...God took them home...it was their time.*

Sound a bit too pat? It should, because that absolute line of theological thought does not stand up to full New Testament scrutiny. It's been said that the best picture of God that anyone will ever have is found in the total person of Jesus. It would take only a cursory study of the sayings, actions, and impact of Jesus to determine that he did not have a malevolent moment in his life. He was a God of grace and love. He wanted to provide the best possible existence for his people, not a capricious ride of questions and insecurities.

The same can be said for God's activity level in recurring temptations. In short, there isn't any activity by God in temptation situations. Satan is the main player in those situations, followed a close second by ourselves. Scripture is explicitly clear about God not being able to abide sin or evil. God does not tempt us to test our faith level or maturity. Satan is active in our temptations in order to disrupt and distract us from embodying genuine faith. His goal is to pull us away from following God with our entirety. God's goal is for us to resist the dynamic temptations of Satan and draw closer to him. God and Satan...never the twain shall meet!

Bottom line: Bad things happen in life. People die, fortunes are lost, and sooner or later, fear and doubt will rear their debilitating heads in every life. The natural order is in place and because of that physical fact, hurricanes, floods, tornadoes, and earthquakes will occur with regularity. You ask, *Where is God in all of this?*

God is patiently waiting to love us through any negative event that comes our way. We can ask why God did not stop the tragedy until we are old, bitter, and broken, but we still won't have the answer. Our only productive and edifying response is to keep trusting God. Embrace his love. Appreciate his care. Thank him for his mind-boggling unconditional love.

On our darkest of days, that tack will bring a ray of hope that death itself can't dash. We will get stronger. We will endure.

Endurance is the key phrase in James' first statements to the dispersed believers. Keep trusting God no matter the cost and you will grow in spiritual strength and power. Trials will come, but you can endure. Trials will no doubt come, but you can ultimately win the prize.

> Therefore we also, since we are surrounded by so great a cloud of witnesses, let us lay aside every weight, and the sin which so easily ensnares us, and let us run with endurance the race that is set before us, looking unto Jesus, the author and finisher of our faith, who for the joy that was set before Him endured the cross, despising the shame sat down at the right hand of the throne of God. (Hebrews 12:1-2 [NKJV])

Prayer

Father...help us to see the joy in all of life. From the morning sun to the evening glow, may we see your purpose for our lives...may we feel your presence in both the good and the bad experiences. Persecution will come...pain will be made known...temptation will invade, yes Father, all sorts of evil may be visited upon us. Lead us to endure...lead us to be victorious...may we be more than conquerors due to your ever abiding love and commitment to us. Can anything separate us from your love? No, your promises are clear. We praise you for your promises. May we love you in return with the same fervor and intensity and passion.

1. List three things that come to mind when the word trials is mentioned.

_____

_____

_____

_____

_____

_____

2. Give the three components that define trial by New Testament standards.

_____

_____

_____

_____

_____

_____

3. Define joy as you would to a non-Christian.

_____

_____

_____

_____

_____

_____

4. In one sentence, state how a person can be joyful while in the midst of trials (see also Romans 15:13 and Ephesians 3:14-21).

_____

_____

_____

_____

_____

5. Describe the differences between the trials of today and those faced by the early believers.

_____

_____

_____

_____

_____

_____

6. Describe your views on God's activity level in daily life.

_____

_____

_____

_____

_____

_____

7. Describe your views on Satan's activity level in daily life.

_____

_____

_____

_____

_____

_____

8. Describe an instance where perseverance or endurance through a trial made you stronger.

_____

_____

_____

_____

_____

_____

9. Read James 1:2-4 and create your own personal prayer.

_____

_____

_____

_____

_____

_____

Is My Wisdom Showing?

James 1:5-8

How many times have you heard the line, *Well, one thing just led to another.* By looking at life sequentially, one would have to admit that one thing usually does lead to another. The question is, *What exactly does one thing lead to?* Is it good or bad? Positive or negative?

James is building momentum in chapter one to show his displaced readers that adversity properly dealt with can lead to a multitude of positives. The completeness he addresses in verse 4 is solidified in verse 5 as he deals with wisdom:

> But let patience have its perfect work, that you may be perfect and complete, lacking nothing. If any of you lacks wisdom, let him ask of God, who gives to all liberally and without reproach, and it will be given to him. (1:4-5 [NKJV])

Trials should lead us closer to God. How does one normally approach God? With fear and trembling? It would depend upon what one has been into, I suppose, but if God is approached as spiritual father, prayer is the normal route of engagement. There is an excellent chance that after spending time with God in prayer, one will feel better about life. Whether we realize it or not, by the very act of engaging in prayer we are the beneficiaries of wisdom. Change will also follow a genuine encounter with God. Increased wisdom, a by-product of genuine communion with God, is evidence of this positive change.

So what's the difference between wisdom and I.Q.? Brains are brains, right? We often refer to older people as wise and are prone to say that someone is *wise for their age.* Leonardo da Vinci is widely considered to have held the "most complete" brain in all of history.

The average person is dominant in one side or the other, either the right or left side of the brain. Leonardo da Vinci was the consummate mathematician (left) and gifted artist (right). He was a genius in the classic analytical sense, as well as in the creative areas. He was in actuality whole-brained, but was he also wise?

James would say that the wisdom he is advocating is spiritual in nature, and is actually a spiritual gift. It doesn't come from self-study or from genetic I.Q. It is a free gift from God, simply for the asking. The potential for this wisdom comes with the Holy Spirit upon salvation. As salvation develops, God will grant an unlimited supply of supernatural wisdom to those who seek it. It will not, however, be thrown at individuals as beads are at a Mardi Gras parade. It's not that easy or capricious. Once sought and bestowed, one's potential for growing in this wisdom is exponential. So the answer to the aforementioned question, "Was da Vinci wise?" would depend on your definition of wise. According to James, da Vinci would rank as wise only if he faithed God and sought wisdom from above. By utilizing this mode of thinking, there are profound differences between wisdom and I.Q.

James was advocating that the dispersed believers rely on this *spiritual* sense to deal with the realities of their new existence, to discern and then follow God's specific will for their lives, and to continue to develop spiritually (1:4). Again, this approach stands to reason. A dispersed and persecuted believer could not possibly be successful in faithing God if they continually questioned his will, his motives, or their own personal plight. To be successful they had to hold fast to their faith and believe that God was ultimately in control of their situation. This is where the gift of wisdom becomes all-important. Without the utilization of the gift of spiritual wisdom, one would be left with only the natural elements with which to make decisions. This could literally destroy a new believer in the situations relative to the first century. Human wisdom and intelligence would most assuredly lead to resignation and further flight for the oppressed and persecuted. History has shown that it has taken much less negative resistance for a person of faith to "cash in their chips" (see John 18:15-18).

History confirms that these new believers did indeed trust God, and they were successful in the face of great adversity. James tells us that the root of such victory is found in relying on the gift of spiritual wisdom. This type of wisdom is the direct conduit to discerning and then following God's will. Successful (spiritual) navigation through life depends upon this "otherworldly" approach. Actually, it seems such a simple equation for success. If this is a true assessment, then why do so many people mess it up so readily?

SIMPLE! One cannot discern God's will if one does not have spiritual wisdom, and one cannot receive wisdom if one is not drawing close to God. It is a classic issue of proximity. If one isn't seeking to draw close to God as a lifestyle element, there really is no hope of truly ascertaining God's will.

The prerequisites are so simple. We are to draw close to God, worshiping and focusing upon him as our dynamic center. After that, simply ask...simply seek. God is expecting no less from us. *Let him ask* in verse 6 is actually from an imperative Greek verb that translates as a command. Apparently God did not see the need for close communion and spiritual wisdom to be options. Obviously for many believers it is just that, something opted in and out of at will. "Our will" of course.

This brings up a new set of issues and problems. Ever wondered what God thinks of believers who so readily move in and out of relationships with him? It's easy to assume that it causes him pain, just as earthly parent/child relationships often example. Here's a *grace* element in action; he is pained by our fickleness, yet he doesn't lash out. In verse 5 we are told that when we do draw close and seek wisdom, he will bestow it without reproach. Translated best, *reproach* means to severely reprimand. God does not reprimand us for playing our relationship with him like a yo-yo. It seems that his love for us is simply too strong for that. There's a ton to be learned from that fact alone.

However, there are stipulations and guidelines for receiving wisdom. One must approach God with pure motives. One must be genuine in their contrite approach. Verse 8 tells us that we must approach God in faith without any doubting. We must be genuine in our reasoning for asking for the wisdom from the beginning. With that same genuine spirit, we must trust God to deliver. In short, we must be spiritually genuine and have full belief that God is genuine as well.

This is a flunkable test! Whether we believe that God won't supply our need due to personal unworthiness or a lack of power, negative belief reigns regardless. James calls this being *double-minded* and *unstable* (1:8). A description of a lightweight being tossed to and fro by the wind and waves is certainly no compliment. Yet it is a mantle worn at times by many believers. Ever wonder if anyone has ever gotten spiritually seasick from all the tossing to and fro on the waves?

The main theme of these verses is the attainment of spiritual wisdom. Wisdom from God is at the epicenter of our formative needs. Spiritually we are impotent without this pivotal wisdom. So James is urging his readers to *do the right thing* in ascertaining and then utilizing supernatural wisdom. For the first-century believer it was necessary to survive, and for today's believer it is necessary to progress. This being the case, a litmus test is available for all believers today: *Is my wisdom showing?* Sure you want the answer to that one? Of course you do...in Christ we are simply a prayer away from a new beginning. Wisdom for a prayer? The exchange rate on that transaction is absolutely priceless!

Prayer

Father...lead me to be wise. Help me to see that relying upon my own understanding is ultimately selfish, futile, and dangerous. May I draw closer to you, seeking your attention, seeking wisdom. May I be progressive...moving forward...seeking to do your will. May this wisdom protect me from sin and become a light for needy people to see. May wisdom begat wisdom and the world change because of it. Light...power...wisdom, be all three for me.

1. Describe ways in which trials in life could lead you closer to God.

_____

_____

_____

_____

_____

_____

2. Describe ways in which trials in life could lead you away from God.

_____

_____

_____

_____

_____

_____

3. James would say that *wisdom* is the key to moving closer to God when in the midst of trials. Define wisdom as you would to a non-Christian.

_____

_____

_____

_____

_____

_____

4. What are the basic differences between wisdom and I. Q.?

_____

_____

_____

_____

_____

Is My Wisdom Showing?

5. *God gives generously to all, without finding fault.* What do these words mean to you?

_____

_____

_____

_____

_____

_____

6. We are encouraged to ask of God and then to believe without doubt. Doubt what?

_____

_____

_____

_____

_____

_____

7. How does being *genuine* affect this situation?

_____

_____

_____

_____

_____

_____

8. Describe a person who is *double-minded.*

_____

_____

_____

_____

_____

_____

9. Describe the benefits of supernatural wisdom.

_____

_____

_____

_____

_____

_____

_____

10. Read James 1:5-8 and create your own personal prayer.

_____

_____

_____

_____

_____

_____

_____

If I Were a Rich Man...

James 1:9-11

What is it about money that so often makes people so crazy? It seems that throughout history, money and material wealth have been motivating forces. Is it just me, or does it seem that people of material means always fare better in most all aspects of life than do people of poverty? It stands to reason, I suppose, with wealth being what it is in society. While Sir Francis Bacon was resolute that knowledge equaled power, most people seem to prefer cash!

How about the believer? Was James saying that money was but filthy lucre? A pagan's folly? A wasteful diversion? No, and neither did Jesus, Paul, Peter, or any other person identified with Scripture. James seems to be entertaining a genuine dichotomy in these verses, that material wealth did indeed come with its own unique pitfalls and problems and that poverty was not as bad as it was widely refuted to be. So money is not the evil of all evils, and poverty is actually a blessing? I realize that we are supposed to be viewing much of life through a glass darkly and all, but this truly seems to be a stretch, doesn't it? No, it just needs context.

James was actually a bit hard on the rich throughout his letter, usually to make bold points. He had a tendency to equate the rich with non-faith people, those who made a god of their material possessions. Obviously this line of thought makes sense when considering the whole of New Testament writings. But let's face it, poverty was not usually thought to be a reason for celebration. In the traditional sense, this was not the intent of James either. He was referring to the transcendent nature of poverty.

Staying true to the *trials* theme, James was stating that poverty was a trial to be endured, just as riches were. This signified that poverty was temporal in nature, which was certainly great news to these dispersed believers. Remember that due to their faith they generally lost their livelihoods, their homes, and their potential for a normal life. Following Christ in that period was an all-inclusive commitment for most new converts. But poverty was not distinctly related to accepting Christ entirely. There were other factors leading to pervasive levels of poverty in that age.

There was an unbalanced socioeconomic structure in place throughout the first-century world. There was a distinct upper class and an equally distinct lower class, but hardly a middle class at all. There were artisans and craftsmen who could be linked to a center class, but in light of the obvious differences between upper and lower classes, they would be better classified as lower-lower upper class. It stands to reason that the majority of people would fall toward the lower end of the socioeconomic spectrum. To compound the miseries of rampant poverty were the realities of the Roman and Orthodox Hebrew oppression. Add it all up, and there was a high percentage of new believers who were all but destitute.

So in light of all of the inequities and oppression that led to many or most of his readers being in great poverty (not to mention fully dispersed), James calls on them to rejoice. He is in essence saying to these troubled people, "Glory in your high position," "Be proud." The Greek word for *glory* is often translated *boast* or *rejoice*. *Rejoice*, even *boast* over your high position. Exactly what high position would that be? This would seem to be a major social paradigm leap. But here's where the theology kicks in.

The cultural definition of the day would demand that poverty was nothing to be proud of, much less a cause for celebration. In fact, Hebrew culture taught that poverty was a sign of God's disfavor, just as it taught the inverse belief that wealth was a sign of God's love and favor. James was saying no, quite the opposite in fact. He advocated looking at poverty through the lens of faith. By doing so, and by applying spiritual wisdom, a person could see past the circumstances of the present and see a glimpse of God's ordained tomorrow. This was a huge plus for these dispersed believers who were on the run and in the grip of poverty. There was a hope and there was a future. This present state of chaos was but temporary. God was indeed in ultimate control!

James had news for the other side as well. While the news was excellent for the poverty-laden believers, it was not encouraging for the rich. What goes around comes around, as they say. James was telling the ungodly rich that they shouldn't become too smug about their seemingly positive circumstances. "Seemingly" is definitely the operative word in this case. Their circumstances were portrayed as temporary and fleeting.

> Let the lowly brother glory in his exaltation, but the rich in his humiliation, because as a flower of the field he will pass away. For no sooner has the sun risen with a burning heat than it withers the grass; its flowers, and its beautiful appearance perishes. So the rich man also will fade away in his pursuits. (1:9-11 [NKJV])

Flowers and grass withering from the scorching heat! The beauty of a flower perishing! Fading away! Bummer! Sobering reality was exactly the hoped for end result of his writing. This fading away and scorching motif did indeed point out the absolute temporal nature of our earthly existence. *Here today and gone tomorrow!* It also details the eternal importance of to whom or what we give our allegiance. Cash, even large amounts of it, will go only as far as the grave. It is not uncommon to hear that someone is "set for life" due to vast material wealth. The question is, "Which life?" There are two, you know!

One obvious positive lesson that can be learned from this section is this: "If the poor and oppressed look with a future view, past their immediate circumstances, they can see their exalted place in God's eternal economy and social structure." The persecution of the day could not change God's secure future for his people; neither could mega-poverty. This is what these first-century believers most needed to hear.

Of course, there is an inverse morale at play here as well. Verse 10 in the Phillips translation sums it up: "The rich may be proud that God has shown him his spiritual poverty." God loves the rich as much as the poorest of the poor. The problem is, as detailed by the whole of the New Testament, that many rich people never look past their personal riches to discover God's love or their own spiritual plight. It would be difficult for a person to see his or her own spiritual poverty when at the same time reveling in their material riches. One doesn't necessarily mirror the other. So false security can lead a person to a brutal ending.

So what can we take from this section of James' letter?

1. Poverty is indeed a trial to be endured, but so is wealth.
2. As with other trials, poverty can be endured by embracing providential love.
3. If we place prime emphasis upon material possessions, losses will ensue.
4. God's ultimate has both a present tense and a future tense.
5. Material riches are a present-tense entity only.

> As the poor brother forgets all his earthly poverty, so the rich brother forgets all his earthly riches. (Lenski, 535)

Prayer

I am rich, wealthy beyond all measure, yet so totally undeserving. I possess grace, peace, love, patience, understanding, and full forgiveness. May I never succumb to the fallacies of material gain that so often and easily corrupt. May I forever faith you Father, realizing just how blessed I am because of your love for me. What shall separate me from your love? Absolutely nothing unless I allow it to take place. Allow me to see past the circumstances of today and, in the process, see your glorious future. A future of richness and fulfillment.

1. In a nutshell, what is today's societal view of money and material wealth?

_____

_____

_____

_____

_____

_____

2. In these verses, how would you describe the view of James concerning money and material wealth?

_____

_____

_____

_____

_____

_____

3. It's obvious that poverty was a trial to be endured by the early believers, yet James counted riches as a trial as well. Explain what you think he means.

_____

_____

_____

_____

_____

_____

4. How could a person of poverty or low social standing take pride or joy in their condition?

_____

_____

_____

_____

_____

_____

5. What do you think James meant when he said that the rich should take pride in their *low position*?

_____

_____

_____

_____

_____

_____

_____

6. In a nutshell, describe the lessons to be learned from verses 10 and 11.

_____

_____

_____

_____

_____

_____

7. While Scripture never actually states that being wealthy is, in and of itself, wrong, it does consistently deal with the potential dangers of wealth. List five dangers of material wealth as you perceive them.

_____

_____

_____

_____

_____

_____

8. Describe what you believe this quote is attempting to convey: *As the poor brother forgets all his earthly poverty, so the rich brother forgets all his earthly riches* (Lenski, 535).

_____

_____

_____

_____

_____

_____

9. Read James 1:9-11 and create your own personal prayer.

_____

_____

_____

_____

_____

_____

_____

Temptation Stands on Every Corner and Calls My Name

James 1:12-18

For the believer, temptation is as much a part of the fabric of life as the air we breathe. It is a constant reality and it is battle worthy. And, as James so fittingly portrays it, temptation is as much a trial to be endured as is persecution. The Greek word *peirasmos*, the noun form of the verb translated "tempted," holds the meaning of "testing," "trying," or "assaying." Out of the three-part definition of trials (session one), this particular element seems to be the most prevalent for today's believer, while direct persecution was the greatest dilemma facing the first-century reader.

James is using a very stark, black and white approach in these verses. He is plainly stating that if a person responds to temptation by seeking out God for power, strength, and wisdom, then he or she can endure the temptation event. If one does not seek out God and responds out of his or her own power or wisdom, chances are that the natural self will win out. If that happens, the person has allowed the natural sin condition to reign and become predominant in his or her life. Obviously, for the believer, one is a positive response, and the other is patently negative. One enhances spiritual development, while the other leads to spiritual decay. One correctly utilizes the gift of spiritual wisdom to combat sin and evil, while the other relies solely on natural wisdom to make choices that turn out to be quite natural. Since this isn't rocket science we are talking about, it's not hard to determine the correct direction that believers should take.

Why is the issue of dealing with temptation so important for the believer to consider? Simply because of the prevalence and absolute influence of temptation. *All God's children gonna face temptation!* Paul wrote in 1 Corinthians 10:13 that everyone will face temptation, even the most spiritual people:

No temptation has overtaken you except such as is common to man. (NKJV)

Even Jesus faced temptation at the hands of Satan, albeit in the biggest mismatch in all of history. Jesus withstood the temptation, proving to us two things: first, temptation can be overcome, and second, it takes spiritual discipline to overcome it. Jesus went into this battle fully prepared. Matthew 4:2 states that Jesus had fasted for forty days and nights before the temptation event. He was engaging in spiritual preparation. Doesn't it stand to reason that if Jesus had to prepare for temptation that we have no prayer of successfully withstanding it without doing the same?

Bottom line: We will be tempted. So it isn't a question of if temptation will occur, or even when it will arrive. The big question for the believer is simply what will be the response to temptation. The "if" and "when" are givens; they are not controlled by the believer. The response, however, is totally in the hands of the believer.

There seem to be two general responses to temptation by believers: One possible response is to claim the power and wisdom that is available to each believer from God, and in so doing, fend off the temptation event. It is an exercise in saying "no" with supernatural power. By choosing this response, one gains in spiritual maturity, wisdom, and strength. This response also keeps intact the spiritual relationship with God.

The other possible response is to give in to the base desires, lusts, or inclinations that temptation feeds off of, and sin. Giving in to temptation is easy and can be both quick and fulfilling. The fulfilling nature of temptation is bound by the natural elements, so in and of itself, it must be short lived. Obviously that is the reason that it returns so often. It becomes a satiation issue. The longer one revels in a pleasure, the more of the pleasure it takes to fully satisfy. So the temptation comes around more often and, after gaining entry, stays longer. Spiritually this is fully detrimental in a number of ways. First and foremost, if a person is entertaining temptation and sin, there is no vacancy for God. Since God can't abide with sin, *something's gotta go*! That would be God in this case, yet it would actually be the person moving away from God and not the other way around. A volitional acceptance of sin is a volitional denial of God's predominant place in one's life. Believe it or not, it gets worse. The longer a person remains away from God and in the active presence of natural sin, the more they begin to display the symptoms of spiritual decay. While most believe that one's salvation is secure, even with spiritual decay in force (Luke 15:11-24), the picture is still quite ugly. Picture a fish out of the water. The longer it stays out of its designed element, the closer it comes to death. It is not happy, not fully functional, and sooner or later it fully succumbs. Then it begins to smell even worse than it did when alive. Get the picture? Decay is decay. If we choose to live in an element of natural sin and away from God, we will embody that which is natural. Spiritually, we will stink!

Another issue often surfaces when a believer opts to give in to temptation: BLAME! Call it being human, weak, or foolish, but people do tend to blame someone or something for their failures. THIS IS A NO RESPONSIBILITY ZONE! It gets worse. People seek to blame someone or something not only for being tempted, but also for their succumbing to the temptation in the first place. Adam and Eve were co-conspirators in the first "blame game" as recorded in Genesis 3.

Adam: "The woman whom you gave to be with me, she gave me from the tree and I ate."

Eve: "The serpent deceived me and I ate."

Eve blamed the serpent while Adam blamed her, and then Adam took a shot at God.

James seemed to sense that if people normally opt to blame other people or things for their failures, then a natural transgression would be to blame God as well. After all, God can't be seen or audibly heard. Blame God and hope for the best later. Unfortunately, Hebrew teaching did not assist the first-century readers of this book either. Rabbis often taught that God dealt equally in all sides of life, both in the good events and the bad. Therefore, if temptation was the issue, God may have initiated the temptation. An old Hebrew saying goes like this, "God provides the favor and blessing.... He tempts and tests."

James is providing a hard and fast "no" to the very idea that God would tempt his people. James emphatically states that God does not put people into situations in order for them to prove their strength or commitment. The school of thought that portrays God as both tempter and tester conflicts with the belief that God wants the very best possible existence for his followers. Plus, God simply cannot abide with sin.

MacArthur's New Testament commentary on James cites four proofs that God cannot entice evil:

A. The Nature of Evil (1:13b)
"For God cannot be tempted by evil, and He Himself does not tempt anyone" (47).

B. The Nature of Man (1:14)
"But each one is tempted when he is carried away and enticed by his own lust" (49).

C. The Nature of Lust (1:15-16)
"Then when lust was conceived, it gives birth to sin, and when sin is accomplished it brings forth death. Do not be deceived my beloved brothers" (51).

D. The Nature of God (1:17)
"Every good thing given and every perfect gift is from above, coming down from the Father of Lights, with whom there is no variation or shifting shadow" (54).

There are a few obvious truths evidenced here that should solidify the reality that God cannot be factored into the sin/temptation equation. First, God cannot be associated with evil because God and evil are mutually incompatible. In verse 13b, the Greek adjective used carries the meaning, "without the capacity for temptation." God is both above and beyond the possibility of temptation on any level. Second, evil is an operational force with great power and constancy. In verses 15 and 16, a metaphor is used to convey lust as a mother who gives birth to an offspring known as sin. As bad apples go, the only destiny for this child is death and destruction. The point is clear; lust will open the way for concrete sin, which brings about spiritual decay, and if left unattended, death. Third, we as humans are often our own worst enemy. We are creatures naturally prone to sin, literally born into a sin condition that we can't rise above without God's help. If God is our only hope, then it stands to reason that he can't be part of the problem.

Yes, temptation will be a constant foe for all believers throughout life. Temptation does not rest or take vacations (especially at the beach). Temptation recognizes weaknesses and is single-minded in its pernicious assaults. It cannot, however, hold sway over spiritual power. God, as described in verse 17, is the Father of Lights. This ancient Jewish title conveys God as creator or giver of light (sun, moon, and stars). Stars burn out, and eventually so will the sun and moon, but the author of these lights will continue forward (see Exodus 3:1-14).

Herein lies the strength and hope for all people. Temptation is absolutely no match for God's people if they are willing to rise above their human condition and accept, exercise, and focus on the power of God for their daily lives.

> For I am persuaded that neither death nor life, nor angels nor principalities nor powers, nor things present nor things to come, nor height nor depth, nor any other created thing, shall be able to separate us from the love of God which is in Christ Jesus. (Romans 9:38-39 [NKJV])

Prayer

Father...for my weaknesses I repent. For my repeated trips back to my former life, I ask for forgiveness. For so easily trading time in the light for a selfish sojourn in the darkness, I stand ashamed. I claim you as my Father of Light. I accept your power to stand strong in the face of temptation. I say yes to power. Lead me to be pure, and may my life be a testament to your grace.

1. Why do you think that believers are tempted?

_____

_____

_____

_____

_____

_____

_____

2. Why do you think people often believe that God is involved in their temptation?

_____

_____

_____

_____

_____

_____

3. Scripture is quite clear on the fact that God does not tempt people. It is also equally as clear about the root of all temptations. What is it?

_____

_____

_____

_____

_____

_____

4. Verse 15 gives an analogy of the life cycle as related to sin. In your own words, explain it.

_____

_____

_____

_____

_____

_____

5. Why do people tend to blame someone or something for personal failures?

_____

_____

_____

_____

_____

_____

6. If God does not tempt people, does he test them?

_____

_____

_____

_____

_____

_____

7. What is the difference?

_____

_____

_____

_____

_____

_____

_____

8. We are naturally prone to sin. We will consistently face temptations. Yet we have hope in Christ to become stronger and more complete. Describe what we must do to become both stronger and more complete in the face of temptation.

_____

_____

_____

_____

_____

9. Read James 1:12-18 and create your own personal prayer.

_____
_____
_____
_____
_____
_____
_____

You Have Two Ears but Only One Mouth... Ever Wonder Why?

James 1:19-21

Sticks and stones may break my bones, but words can never hurt me.

Yeah, right. *Liar, liar pants on fire* is more like it! The use of words literally runs the spectrum. Words can uplift, praise, and create positives. Words can also be neutral. However, words can be used to inflict pain, bring hurt, and for all manner of malicious purposes.

The correct words used in the proper circumstances can motivate, bring forth laughter, and progress love. Words spoken with little or no thought or regard to how they will be received can bring discouragement, compound disgrace, and increase insecurities.

No wonder James and other biblical writers made such a big deal about the dangers of speech. A possible quagmire exists for everyone with a tongue each and every time the mouth opens. Pending stress or fatigue levels or, more importantly, spiritual shape, the outcome of speech could go in any direction. Even people of faith face this dilemma on a regular basis.

Check out what James writes in chapter 3:

> But no man can tame the tongue. It is an unruly evil, full of deadly poison. With it we bless our God and with it we curse men, who have been made in God's image. Out of the same mouth proceeds blessing and cursing. My Brothers, these things ought not to be so. (3:8-10 [NKJV])

When asked how he responds to teammates who regularly curse, A. C. Green, NBA player and devout Christian responded, "I ask them if they kiss their mama with that same mouth!"

James believed in personalizing the problem as well. He was constant in his admonitions to his readers to live out the faith in complete ways. If they were to be a positive influence in reaching people for Christ, they had to first embody the gospel that they professed. In earlier verses, James urged the readers to embody their faith while dealing with trials and temptations. Now he is moving toward interpersonal activities, specifically speech habits and their all around effects. One could make the case that James is on a course of direct assault against the dangers of a tongue out of control.

Small wonder, huh? In later verses, James characterizes the tongue as "a fire," "a world of iniquity," and as "a defiler of the whole body." No glowing endorsements there, but why should there be? Take a look in the memory's mirror: Have you ever said something so wrong that you wanted to suck the words back into your mouth? Can you recollect throwing a fit and acting like a fool? Ever had a cursing problem? Have words of stinging critique disguised as gossiping ever escaped your internal censors? How about the lucky lot who witnessed the sad deeds, what were their reactions? Embarrassment? Pity? Pain?

Since we are on a memory groove here, have you ever wondered if someone has ever had problems reconciling your Christian faith with your actions? Uh-oh! Precisely, this is what James is majoring on in this section. He could have titled this section, "How Not To Be a Verbal Hypocrite." Being a hypocrite and being a bad witness of the gospel are exactly the dangers that James is warning against. So he gives his readers a concise lifestyle equation to help them keep control of their tongues and their reputations. This equation is as profound as it is simple: *Be quick to listen, slow to speak, slow to anger.*

There is a downward progression implicit in this equation. If one speaks with haste and ignores listening, anger could possibly result. One mistake can lead to another, and the next thing you know, sin is afoot. The more one speaks, the bigger the margin for error.

In the multitude of words, sin is not lacking (Proverbs 10:19 [NKJV]).

Listen first...listen attentively, next
    Consider the response...choose the words carefully...check the tenor, tone and pace, next
    Then, and only then, make the decision as to how to respond.

Of course anger and other negative responses are ready options in communicating. Since it would be hard to make a case for negative responses being uplifting or edifying, these should be the rarest of all responses for the believer. The Greek word for anger can be translated as *wrath, indignation,* or *vengeance.* None of these sounds remotely Christlike. To the contrary, Paul wrote, "God did not appoint us to wrath [anger], but to obtain salvation through our Lord Jesus Christ" (1 Thessalonians 5:9 [NKJV]). In Colossians 3:8, we are instructed to remove "anger, wrath, malice, blasphemy, and filthy language" from our lives. Pretty much covers it as far as words and negative actions go.

Paul took the positive tack in Philippians 4:8, "Whatever things are true, whatever things are noble, whatever things are just, whatever things are pure, whatever things are lovely, whatever things are of good report,...meditate on these things" (NKJV).

The instruction here is to concentrate on the positive and the true. This tack will lead to a life dominated by the positive, while anything else will provide entry to the slippery slope of negativism. Negativity breeds negativity at what seems like exponential speed, and it's rare that anything positive could come of that choice.

Plus, anger and other assorted negative actions can be detrimental to a person's health. Again and again, anger and its cousin "stress" have been proven to do internal damage in insidious ways. In *Anger Is a Choice,* Tim Lahaye and Bob Phillips chronicle earlier work by the ground-breaking duo of Freidman and Rosenman on the not-so-positive events that occur internally as anger builds and is played out:

Hypothalamus and pituitary glands dump hormones into the bloodstream
Breathing rate increases
Adrenalin flows are dramatically increased
Digestion and elimination slow down
Pupils dilate
Blood sugar level rises
Blood pressure increases (especially dangerous for the hypertensive)
Muscles tighten and blood clots faster
Cumulative stress response plays out (42).

It's hard to believe that dying young could be a productive event for the Kingdom of God. Same goes for experiencing a stroke or being stressed out to the max. Could these possibly be events that God could bless? Not likely, but the question does arise, "Didn't Jesus get angry?" The answer to that pointed question is, "Yes." Jesus did indeed become angry; in fact, he went quite wild. As recorded in Mark 11:15-17, Jesus went ballistic over people using the Temple Court as a flea market of sorts. He overturned the vendors' tables and seats and basically ran them off. Quite a sight to behold, Jesus kicking over tables and flinging merchandise! On the surface, it could lead a run-of-the-mill believer to feel better about personal outbursts, but it shouldn't. By digging deeper into these verses, a pattern emerges, one that does not condone run-of-the-mill angry outbursts. What really made Jesus so upset? Whatever happened to "all things noble and true"? To Jesus, what he did was about "noble and true" issues. His anger was focused on something directly related to the Kingdom of God. These (hopefully) pagan vendors were cheapening the Temple of God with their commerce, showing disrespect to a place of worship and prayer. It would be hard to get more "Kingdom" oriented than that!

So Jesus became demonstrably angry over a violation to the Kingdom of God. What's the last thing you became unglued over? Traffic? Burnt toast? Stock prices? Starving children? Homeless people dying in the streets? People with AIDS? People dying without Christ? Kingdom issue...or not?

James' lifestyle equation is actually a "faith-style" equation. To best relate to others and to "be the gospel" to the world, we should follow his advice:

Listen first...listen attentively, next
    Consider the response...choose the words carefully...check the tenor, tone and pace, next
    Then, and only then, make the decision as to how to respond.

Will anger be the response? Why not let the Kingdom decide!

Prayer

Father...lead me to be a listener. May I listen attentively, putting the needs of the other person first. May I respond with your words...in kindness and in peace...imparting grace to the world. I apologize for my anger and the damage to the Kingdom that it has certainly caused. I am sorry for my negative bend and my habit of judging people and circumstances. Forgive me and lead me to be forgiveness for other people. May I come in peace and go in peace...and may I have an eye and a heart for your Kingdom.

1. Describe three ways that words can be used in positive ways.

_____

_____

_____

_____

_____

_____

2. Describe the opposite, three ways that words can be used in negative and unproductive ways.

_____

_____

_____

_____

_____

_____

3. Describe potential dangers associated with speaking with haste.

_____

_____

_____

_____

_____

_____

4. Describe potential benefits associated with being *quick to listen*.

_____

_____

_____

_____

_____

_____

5. How would being *quick to listen* and *slow to speak* change the communication dynamics between people?

_____

_____

_____

_____

_____

6. Describe ways in which overcoming anger would improve all facets of life.

_____

_____

_____

_____

_____

_____

7. Think back. Have you ever become angry and done things you wish you hadn't done? Describe the ways you may have damaged your Christian witness.

_____

_____

_____

_____

_____

8. The story of Jesus becoming demonstrably angry is found in Mark 11:15-17. Read these verses and contrast his anger from your own personal episodes. What are the major differences?

_____

_____

_____

_____

_____

9. Describe five concrete examples of *getting rid of all moral filth and the evil that is so prevalent* (verse 21).

_____

_____

_____

_____

_____

_____

10. Read James 1:19-21 and create your own personal prayer.

_____

_____

_____

_____

_____

_____

6 Playing Favorites with Favorites

Favorite is one of the most used words in the English language. Don't believe it? Pay attention and you'll hear it used often.

Pizza's my favorite food!
What's your favorite color?
Hey, that's my favorite song!
My favorite movie of all time is...
Fall is my favorite season.

The list could go on forever. We are definitely into "favorites," and I'm no exception. Basketball is my favorite sport. Pete Maravich is my all-time favorite player, with Wilt Chamberlain a close second. Bonhoeffer is my favorite faith writer, and blue is my favorite color. England is my favorite country to visit, and mysteries are my favorite use of words. Get the picture? Favorites rule! But why? Why do we like and, therefore, use that word so much? Possibly because it stakes a claim to something, in a way inferring ownership. It personalizes things for us and gives us identity. It is also quite concrete. More than anything, however, our favorites provide a look into what makes us who we are. They are quite informing.

But the word *favorite* has more than one meaning and connotation. While it can signify something we enjoy to the greatest degree, it can also define the practice of special or preferential treatment. The noun "partiality" elicits the notion of showing favoritism. This definition describes the pernicious activity that James was attacking in these verses: *Brothers, do not hold the faith of our Lord Jesus Christ with partiality* (2:1 [NKJV]). Historically, this type of treatment was constant throughout Hebrew history. In effect, the Hebrews did not fully follow through on their assigned duties as the chosen people. That designation is often confused with a "favored status" relationship. While it is obvious that God did have a special place for the Jews, it is also clear that they were chosen to fulfill a role. A huge job description came with being the chosen of God; they were given the role of reconciling the world to God. Tough assignment? The *Mission Impossible* guys never had a job so difficult. However, the job was doable. The Hebrews simply did not get it done. One limitation they had was the feeling that other people were inferior and simply did not measure up. Of course they didn't measure up; that's why they needed a personal relationship with God! It's difficult to reach someone if you don't care at all for them. That is pernicious favoritism at work.

Only an Old testament problem? Not by a long shot. James, Peter, and Paul wrote on the subject, and Jesus taught about it.

> In truth I perceive that God shows no partiality. (Acts 10:34a [NKJV])

> Now the multitude of those who believed were of one heart and one soul; neither did anyone say that any of the things he possessed was his own, but they had all things in common. (Acts 4:32 [NKJV])

> For there is no partiality with God. (Romans 2:11 [NKJV])

> Knowing that whatever good anyone does, he will receive the same from the Lord, whether he is slave or free. And you masters, do the same things to them, giving up threatening, knowing that your own master also is in heaven, and there is no partiality with him. (Ephesians 6:8-9 [NKJV])

> There is neither Jew nor Greek, there is neither slave nor free, there is neither male nor female; for you all are one in Christ Jesus. (Galatians 3:28 [NKJV])

Old Testament writers also dealt with this unspiritual practice:

> You shall do no injustice in judgment; you shall not be partial to the poor, or defer to the great. (Leviticus 19:15 [RSV])

> He who mocks the poor insults his maker. (Proverbs 17:5 [RSV])

Obviously, for much of mankind's history, preferences have been extended for people of power, material substance, and position. It is basically a part of the relational fabric of personal living. Sadly, the inverse is a subsequent reality. Condescension to the poor, to the "have nots," is also a practical reality.

James was saying two things about the practice of showing favoritism:

- It is clearly unspiritual and has no place in the faith community.
- It really makes little sense to engage in this practice.

As to favoritism and partiality being unspiritual, James wanted the believers to know that cultural definitions often do not mesh with spiritual or faith definitions. Culturally it was fine to show distinctions between people, no matter the root of these differences. In the faith community, however, there was no place for accepting this cultural practice. In fact, Jesus made it clear that believers should be visibly and demonstrably different from those who are outside of the faith. Jesus came as the ultimate equalizer. He came to be the bridge between God and his creation for the purpose of full reconciliation. The church, therefore, was to continue the mission. How could it if this practice was tolerated? How could the church be, in effect, Christ for the world, if no one could tell the difference between the world and the church? Hence the problem that James was addressing.

The example that he gave could have been a genuine occurrence, or it could have been purely hypothetical. Arguments also exist about the exact nature of the event. Stulac portrays the two most likely possibilities for the gathering this way:

> The traditional understanding has been that the meeting is a gathering for worship, with non-Christians visitors present. A second and more recently advocated possibility is that the meeting is a judicial assembly of the church, and that the rich and poor individuals are both members of the religious community who are involved in a dispute to be adjudicated (90).

While the interpretation will always be mixed on these points, I concur with Douglas Moo that it was an assembly for the purpose of settling a dispute between members (89). Whether it was hypothetical or genuine in occurrence really isn't material to the lesson to be learned in this section. Used properly, it can drive home a solid point.

The story is of two clearly different classes of people who enter the assembly. One is obviously wealthy, replete with upscale clothes and gold rings (note the plural). These adornments depict a person of both means and stature. The other person is described as wearing basically rags. One early version defines his apparel as "filthy, sordid raiment." His social position is a slam dunk to determine.

As they entered, it appears that the assembled believers were transfixed on the rich man. The Greek words translated *special attention* mean to gaze upon and observe with admiration and special reverence. It must also mean "go to the head of the class" because that's what happened next. The rich man was shown to a seat of honor. In effect, people were falling all over themselves to make the rich man feel honored. What happened to the poor guy? He was being gazed upon as well, albeit for very different reasons. He was told to get his shabby self over to the corner (author's biased paraphrase). Phillips paraphrases it this way: *If you must sit, sit on the floor* (480).

Are the differences showing yet? Obviously! Absolutely! Completely! Now you're hoping that this *was* a hypothetical event, huh? Preference for the outwardly wealthy was in play, which made this assembly no different from the Jerusalem Rotary Club.

The lesson here is stark: If God doesn't show favoritism, then neither can his church.

James was also inferring that the practice of favoring the rich actually made very little sense. For the dispersed, persecuted believers of the first century, this practice was quite illogical. They were using the cultural model of value in respecting material wealth, when it was the materially wealthy that were partially to blame for making their lives so difficult. "Are these not the people who oppress you, drag you into court, and blaspheme the very name of God?" (Author's paraphrase). The mixing of cultural norms and mores with the radically different tenets of faith in Christ will always provide jumbled results.

James also went on to say that favoring the rich was illogical in light of the consistency of God's nondistinctive love. Does God relate to his people in capricious ways? Does God change the rules at will? No and no. Check out the rich young man who asked Jesus about how to achieve salvation (Luke 18:18-23). God measures people by faith. He shows no distinctions between people(s). *Red*

and yellow, black and white, Jesus loves [all] the little children...
Tertullian wrote: "We must not judge faith by people, but people by
faith."

By dealing with the royal law, James made the message even
more clear.

> If you really fulfill the royal law according to the scripture,
> "you shall love your neighbor as yourself," you do well; but if
> you show partiality, you commit sin, and are convicted by the
> law as transgressors. For whoever shall keep the whole law, and
> yet stumble in one point, he is guilty of all. (2:8-10 [NKJV])

Scripture defines God simply as love. We also know that he is
an equalizer. There are no distinctions with God. Since God is
defined as love and is nondistinctive in his respect for all people,
shouldn't the church live that same way as a practical lifestyle? That
would mean loving people "just because." That would mean that no
class distinctions exist within the community of faith. That would
mean that "unconditional" would be an operative word in all
aspects of relationships. It would also mean living out these lifestyle
tenets with consistency. You know, like God does!

Have you ever wondered about this possibility: if God chose to
discriminate, would we, could we, measure up? Not likely! We are
the beneficiaries of an unconditionally loving God who is not capricious. If God were capricious and changed the rules, we would be
toast. If grace was no longer in effect and we had to earn our salvation, heaven would have a great deal of vacancies!

James is seeking an inward look followed by an outward change.
He was asking the new believers to move away from the cultural
practice of favoritism, partiality, and discrimination, to God's model
of unconditional equality. By the very nature of Scripture, he is forc-
ing us to consider our roles as well.

Laurie Beth Jones wrote of the German Poet Rainer Maria
Rilke, who coined the phrase, "Live the question." In response to
extremely difficult or even seemingly impossible situations, she suggests to "live the question" (269). Perhaps that is what we should do
to combat our human nature and the cultural norm in regard to
partiality and making distinctions. There will always be "hard-to-
like" people in the world. Cultural differences will always abound.
There will always be both the rich and the poor taking up space on
our planet. And there will always be the royal law! Our roles have

already been ordained; love them all equally. It's scriptural. There's no getting around it.

> Regardless of the choice...regardless of the question...the answer will always be love.
> Live the question and be the answer.
> If we do, the world's going to be a better place and a whole lot more equal!

Prayer

Father...lead me to be aware of my dislike for people. For my bigotry and my condescension, I am sorry. For looking down on people whom you love, I stand ashamed. Purify my heart and mind and lead me to see people as you do. I also apologize for putting emphasis upon money and position, in my life and in the lives of others. Create in me a fresh heart and a fresh appreciation for all people. You gave me salvation, and you offer it to all, which makes this one giant group outing. May my worldview grow to match yours.

1. With all honesty, list ways you have exhibited prejudice in your life.

_____

_____

_____

_____

_____

_____

2. It's been said that many of today's churches suffer from the "Similarity Syndrome." Why do you think churches seem to attract so many people who are similar?

_____

_____

_____

_____

_____

_____

3. Is this right or wrong? Explain your answer.

_____

_____

_____

_____

_____

_____

4. Do you find it naturally easier to show favoritism to the "haves" over the "have-nots"? Give a brief explanation of your answer.

_____

_____

_____

_____

_____

_____

Playing Favorites with Favorites

5. Why do you think James was saying that the practice of showing favoritism to the rich in the early church wasn't smart?

_____

_____

_____

_____

_____

_____

6. List scriptural examples that prove that God never shows favoritism.

_____

_____

_____

_____

_____

_____

7. What do you think Tertullian meant by these words: *We must not judge faith by people, but people by faith.*

_____

_____

_____

_____

_____

_____

8. In relation to the problem of partiality and favoritism, how would you "live the question" as Rainer Maria Rilke suggests?

_____

_____

_____

_____

_____

9. Describe ways in which life could be different if you lived out the royal law each day.

_____

_____

_____

_____

_____

_____

10. Read James 2:1-13 and create your own personal prayer.

_____

_____

_____

_____

_____

_____

Baptized Nouns or
Baptized Verbs?

James 2:14-28

James has kept a consistent theme alive so far in this letter. Faith has been the operative theme, with obstacles and pitfalls to faith being the practical focal areas. Thus far he has addressed faith while in the midst of trials and temptations, faith and spiritual wisdom, faith and material wealth, faith and righteous living, and faith and favoritism. Next, he moves into an area that has caused a great deal of controversy over the years, faith and works.

Obviously James is not the only New Testament writer to jump into this all-important theological dimension. Paul wrote:

> For by grace you have been saved through faith, and that not of yourselves; it is the gift of God, not of works, lest anyone should boast. For we are His workmanship, created in Christ Jesus for good works, which God prepared beforehand that we should walk in them. (Ephesians 2:8-10 [NKJV])

One of the main tenets of Paul's overall writings is the "saved by faith, not by works" stance. The opposite of this line of thought, "saved by works," or earning salvation, was a theology being taught in early churches. Both Paul and James stood in vivid opposition to this type of teaching. James' stance is point blank in nature, urging his readers to be "doers" of the word and not "hearers" only (1:22-27). Imagine how many people over history have been "hearers" of the gospel, but never more than that. For the gospel to "take," there must be a concrete movement from the previous point in life to a new, altered state. The gospel is transforming in nature. It is not static; it always leads to change if it is genuinely accepted.

You search the scriptures, for in them you think you have eternal life. (John 5:39a [NKJV])

Always learning and never able to come to the knowledge of the truth. (2 Timothy 3:7 [NKJV])

Your Word is a lamp to my feet and a light for my path. (Psalm 119:105 [NKJV])

The idea of a "path" seems to be central to this theological line of thought. Postsalvation, then what? Action would seem to be the proper response. Forward progress is a given for growing faith. It's natural to see action (works) follow a faith experience. *You have faith, and I have works. Show me you faith without your works, and I will show you my faith by my works* (James 2:18 [NKJV]).

BOOM! TAKE THAT! One cannot get any plainer than this approach: "If you have faith, you'll also have accompanying works." Hearing and believing the gospel is simply not enough. One must move beyond simple, basic belief and become the embodiment of that belief. A symbiosis must occur, intertwining belief, faith, and subsequent action. Still not convinced? *You believe there is but one God. You do well. Even the demons believe and tremble!*

James, in 2:19, lowers the boom on any thoughts that plain, simple belief is enough in any form or fashion. *You do well* was not a superlative. It was a slam! If we believe with both heart and mind that Jesus is the Messiah and that God is the one true God, but do not act on that belief, we are equal with demons. Equal with demons! Equal with demons? Either way you design it, exclamation or question, it rings the same.

In 2:26, James describes anyone who believes but does not act on that belief as a foolish person: *For as the body without the spirit is dead, so faith without works is dead also.*

Pure Religion

If our faith is to be real, it must become actualized. There must be tangible, concrete ends to our abstract, supernatural-based faith. Why? For two reasons: First, so we can "do" the gospel. The Great Commission was a job framework for all believers to follow to do God's work here in this life. The plan, or goal, is to reconcile the world to God by way of personal relationship. To do this brings up the second reason, which is "being" the gospel. The concrete application of the gospel will allow nonfaith people to see Christ in our lives. Embodying the tenets of our faith, such as the fruit of the Spirit, will visually and experientially affect other people. "Being" and "doing" naturally fall together, but always in that order. So a question that people of faith should ask is, "What did my faith bring about today?" The answer could be either positive or negative, good or bad. By asking this question, and then honestly answering it, we can determine a great deal about our current spiritual state.

A question that must be asked is, "What defines faith in action?" Is it the reading of the Bible? Is it prayer? Witnessing and evangelism? James stakes a claim for hard and serious definitions for ministry (action) in 1:27:

> Religion that is pure and genuine in the sight of God the Father will show itself by such things as visiting orphans and widows in their distress and keeping oneself uncontaminated by the world. (Phillips)

These words provide a two-fold objective description of faith in action. First, it should be attuned to faith development. Since we are never told to be static in our faith, it stands to reason to be progressive and dynamic (changing). Genuine faith is progressive. The very definition of salvation has a progressive, future orientation (I am saved; I am being saved; I will be saved).

Second, action in the name of faith must occur. During the period of James' writing, orphans were wards of the street. Family customs did not include the taking in of relatives' children who were orphaned. They were, in effect, exiled to the street. Widows were also shown little societal compassion. With no social services or pension possibilities, widows were destined to a sad end. The likelihood of a woman making an honest living was small in that time period, so if a husband died, the wife was all but destitute. A younger widow often had to deal with the added stigma of serious sin in the family, due to the Hebrew belief that sin caused premature death.

James was defining the clearly down and out, as well as true ministry. If you would like a definition of faith in action, stop here. Read no further in James. It's taking care of the lowest factors on society's scale. In that era, it was widows and orphans.... What is it today?

Is your faith defined by action? Or can you look in the mirror and stare into the image of faith's centerpiece? It is one or the other, but never both. Our faith will move forward and subsequently outward, or it will remain static and point inward. One cannot have it both ways.

As if we could feel any worse at this point, James applies an inverse approach in 2:15-17a:

> If a fellow man or woman has no clothes to wear and nothing to eat, and one of you say, "Good luck to you, I hope you'll keep warm and find enough to eat," and yet give them nothing to meet their physical needs, what on earth is the good of that? Yet that is exactly what a bare faith without a corresponding life is like—quite dead. (Phillips)

A vivid example of embracing faith and immediately producing genuine ministry is Zaccheus. After living a life filled with occupational graft and greed, Zaccheus met Jesus both in person and in spirit. His salvation experience resulted in instant conviction and action: *Then Zaccheus stood and said to the Lord, "Look, Lord, I give half of my goods to the poor; and if I have taken anything by false accusation, I restore four-fold"* (Matthew 19:8 [NKJV]).

Zero time wasted there, with salvation spurring ministry action. Being led to doing; faith led to faith-based activity. James goes on to mention both Abraham and Rahab as examples of believers who faithed God and then applied their faith to bold and productive action (works). This active faith is a verb. Webster describes faith in noun form. James describes it as both, but is high only on faith that is a verb. If one's faith is that of a noun, it is, as Phillips puts it, "quite dead."

QUESTION: What percentage of believers today embody "verb" faith?

Sadly, the answer to that question would most likely be low. Look around...think about it...know any Zaccheus-types? Do you know people who are actively ministering to today's *widows and orphans?* Think about people in your church; is their faith-view inward or outward? How about yours? Are these people on a belief-par with trembling demons? Are you?

It seems that "nouns" abound. However, both James and Paul are convinced that Jesus didn't die so we, the people of God, could become a bunch of baptized nouns. He died to open the way for a bunch of verbs to turn the world upside down. The world will be won by verbs, not nouns.

Left up to you, what are the world's chances?

Prayer

Father...lead me to be a living, breathing verb. Lead me away from the temptation to become a noun, simply a static thing. Recreate in me the reality of my faith as defined by action. Allow me to best any and every trembling demon in belief and to be Abraham-like in my commitment to service. Open the door for me to truly make a difference with my grace-buoyed life. May I see it as a gift to be shared through both words and action. And may I never forget how fortunate I am that you love me. Thank you.

1. List the main differences between "saved by faith" and "saved by works."

_____

_____

_____

_____

_____

_____

2. Describe ways in which it's easier to be merely a "hearer" rather than a "doer" of the Word.

_____

_____

_____

_____

_____

_____

3. What must happen for a person to move from merely "hearing" to full-blown "doing" of the Word?

_____

_____

_____

_____

_____

_____

4. In 1:27, James described pure and faultless religion as *looking after orphans and widows in their distress and keeping oneself from being polluted by the world.*

_____

_____

_____

_____

_____

(a) Who or what would represent today's widows and orphans?

_____

_____

_____

_____

_____

_____

_____

(b) Describe ways in which a person can keep from being polluted by the world.

_____

_____

_____

_____

_____

_____

5. Contrast the differences between "verb" faith and "noun" faith.

_____

_____

_____

_____

_____

_____

_____

6. James mentioned Abraham and Rahab as spiritual examples of people who combined faith and action and made profound impact for the Kingdom of God. List other scriptural examples of people who made similar significant impact.

_____

_____

_____

_____

_____

7. Read James 2:14-28 and create your own personal prayer.

_____

_____

_____

_____

_____

_____

Wise as a Three-Dollar Bill

So you're looking to buy a diamond ring for that special someone. You can pay premium dollars for a perfectly cut stone with fire, or you can pay substantially less for a similarly cut cubic zirconium stone (sans the fire!). Hey, who's gonna know?

Interested in a Swiss watch? Famous Swiss precision, true to the second, and what a look! You can shell out the bucks for a certified model, or go to New York and buy a faux model from a guy named Stan on a side street. Hey, who's gonna know?

Well, if you buy from Stan, it's best if you don't let anyone get too close to your new time piece. Upon close inspection, the ruse will be shot. You'll be busted. Everyone's gonna know! Cheapskate! Even worse than cheap, it'll be apparent that you're trying to be something that you aren't prepared to be.

This is the same idea that James conveys in chapter 3. In the earlier verses, he dealt with the pitfalls of being a church leader in the early church. Genuineness is described as the primary attribute of leading a church in the early years. Obviously it remains the same today, but there is a discernible difference between the church of today and the early version. Today there is an enormous amount of leadership, preaching, and teaching aids available. Need a sermon or a great Bible study outline? Buy a book full of them. Need instant help? Hit the Internet. For the early church leader, there was very little to access. So what did they do? They turned to the Holy Spirit and accessed direction from the primary source—which, by the way, is still the best way to get things done!

Genuineness was also an issue in the early church due to the high incidence of false teaching. The New Testament records numerous accounts of "bad theology" at the hands of teachers who infiltrated the early churches. From the Gnostics to the Judaizers to the various Greek pagan groups, the early churches were at risk of being exposed to teaching that was faulty and pernicious.

So it's easy to see why the early leaders needed to be genuine in their commitment and in their teaching. To be genuine, a teacher/leader had to rely upon the Holy Spirit for direction. Sounds like a great idea for the modern church as well!

The idea of genuineness in teaching and the obvious necessity for reliance upon the Holy Spirit leads back to God's promise of wisdom. Beginning in verse 13, James approaches the wisdom argument once again. Who James is talking about in these verses is a major question that arises. Is he continuing his treatise on teachers? While most theologians and scholars think that to be the case, Moo believes in a more universal application. At face value, the teacher section preceding the wisdom one would seem to indicate that he is dealing in just that arena. However, as Moo pointed out, neither the Greek word for *wise* or *knowledge*, is regularly used as a title for teacher. These two terms are used elsewhere in Scripture for leaders in general (Deuteronomy 1:13, 15) and for all of Israel (Deuteronomy 4:6) (131).

The most profitable stance would be to take a universal view of 2:13-18. The interpretation that it applies to all believers bolsters its inherent power to define genuine faith in action (session seven).

There's no getting around the fact that knowledge is primary to life. Over time, how many parents have uttered the words, "If you don't finish your education, you'll never get a good job?" In America we are indoctrinated early with the importance of an education. Bacon nailed it with, "Knowledge is power."

However, it's important to pay attention to how James differentiates between knowledge and wisdom. Again, James portrays wisdom as something neither genetic nor "age-cured." It is, as James defends, a spiritual gift. James is implying that to think otherwise would be foolish. *Who is wise and understanding among you?* (3:13a [NKJV]).

Was this a slam? A rhetorical question? A challenge? Possibly all three, but at the least it was an indictment on the idea that natural wisdom or genetic I.Q. would suffice over God-endowed supernatural wisdom. You have to wonder if anyone raised their hand to answer that stinging question. Who would? Who could? A professing fool, possibly, or someone with zero faith involvement. But it is an answerable question. The answer comes in verse 13b (NKJV):

Let him show by good conduct that his works are done in the meekness of wisdom.

It's as if James is saying, "Alright, so you're wise and understanding; you have a depth of knowledge and are somewhat of an expert. Prove it by your life." This was counter-culture. The Greek mind was ordered, systematic, and philosophical. They were "solvers." James is advocating something quite different. James was asking people to seek wisdom from God, apply that wisdom through a relationship with God, and then solve issues. The Greeks would utilize their natural mental capacities to the fullest, in effect, becoming the masters of their own destiny. James is adding a "middle" element, one that provides for destiny but allocates the role of master to God.

James is making it clear that one cannot go it alone, or rely solely on knowledge or experiential evolution. To be the right type of person and follow God requires a wisdom that transcends both earthly knowledge and experience. The Greeks worked diligently to gain their mental prowess. James is outlining a gift. The labor comes in simply accepting the gift.

James is also outlining the benefits of the gift. Will a person be able to go one-on-one with the Greeks on *Jeopardy* after accepting the gift? Probably not, but the benefits are huge nonetheless. As believers utilize the gift of wisdom, they will grow toward God. As this happens, the way they think, act, and present themselves will change. It is a transition toward holiness. In short, the truly wise and understanding will exhibit their wisdom in ways greatly evident to all.

So what are the hallmarks of the truly wise and understanding? James outlines them in alternating positive and negative adjectival forms.

I. *A Truly Wise Person Would Never Claim to Be Wise*

It's no secret that there are people who have rather high opinions of themselves. Some are even "legends in their own minds." This "I'm-my-own-biggest-fan" syndrome usually comes with a feeling of all-around personal superiority. A truly wise person, however, would never trumpet his or her own wisdom. Why? Because truly wise people see their wisdom as a gift. It was not earned. It was not genetic. It is a gift from God. Solomon wrote: *Acquire wisdom; and with all your acquiring, get understanding* (Proverbs 4:7 [NAS]).

The Roman philosopher Cicero wrote that wisdom is: *The mother of all good things,* and is *The best gift of the gods* (MacArthur, 163).

Solomon urged seeking wisdom from God, which comes with the bonus of understanding. Even Cicero saw that genuine wisdom wasn't inherent in humans; it was an outside gift. Only the truly "unwise" would boast of their wisdom. Sadly, the boasting itself is the biggest giveaway of the type wisdom they embody.

II. *True Wisdom Is Evidenced by Action, Not by Words*

"To the Jews, wisdom was skill in living righteously" (MacArthur, 164). *Let him show it [wisdom] by his good life* (James 3:13b [NIV]).

It's obvious that wisdom is more than wise-sounding words. In a way, wisdom has wheels; it comes with an end result attached. In today's societal nomenclature, *good life* has a connotation of "pleasure-filled" or "prosperous." To James it meant to live righteously and in God's specific and general will. "True wisdom, like real faith, is a vital, practical quality that has as much (or more) to do with the way we live as what we think or say" (Moo, 132).

III. *A Truly Wise Person Is Meek*

Meekness is not a self-ascribed attribute or character trait that you will find on many resumes these days. It was not the *trait du jour* of the first century either. "Meekness was hardly a virtue to be sought after in the minds of most Greeks: it suggested a servile, ignoble debasement" (Moo, 132). Jesus, however, was very big on being meek (Matthew 5:5) and was himself the epitome of New Testament meekness. So how bad can meekness be? Jesus was a "man's man." He was strong, yet tender. He put the needs of other people ahead of his own. In all he did, he defined meekness.

Meekness can also be translated as "gentle" (*praus*), which infers graciousness and tenderness. Jesus was the living definition of all of these. While in English "meek" has a connotation of "weakness," in Greek it is seen as "power under control." This is the definition, or idea, that James has of meekness. It is not being weak; it is being powerful, but under control. The unique thing is the origin of control. The Greek mind would assign control to the individual self. James would say that the source of power is God.

Meekness also leads to selflessness. The only way to achieve this selflessness is to fully understand our standing before God. By placing God first and foremost in all aspects of life, we gain a humility that is evidenced by a lack of pride. This lack of pride equips us to properly deal with other people. So wisdom leads to meekness, which leads to a lack of pride, which leads to humility, which leads to spiritually productive interpersonal relationships. None of this is possible without first seeking supernatural wisdom. It's easy to see why James deals with this area in such volume and detail.

IV. *True Wisdom Leads to Peace*

Do you remember what Jesus said when he appeared to the disciples after his resurrection? Was it, "You knuckleheads! Why didn't you listen to me?" No, he said simply: *Peace be with you* (John 24:36). Jesus gave them what they needed most, peace. As evidenced by these disciples, peace isn't a by-product of one's own human devices. That would be chaos—again, as evidenced by these disciples. Peace is a by-product of the gift of wisdom. It is not attainable in any other manner. It can't be purchased or achieved. It can only be granted.

> But the wisdom that is from above is first pure, then peaceable, gentle, willing to yield, full of mercy and good fruits, without partiality and without hypocrisy. Now the fruit of righteousness is sown in peace by those who make peace. (James 3:17-18 [NKJV])

V. *A Truly Wise Person Is Peace*

Jesus brought peace with him. He embodied peace. Verse 18 lets us know that we should "be" peace as well. Only the gift of supernatural wisdom can create this possibility in us, so to "be" peace, we must first be wise. The opposite is true as well. Without wisdom and subsequent peace, a person will embody nonspiritual character traits. Rather than exhibiting peace, chaos will be evident. Peace allows for joy and patience, but without peace, all one can expect is discontent and impatience. These are the end results of earthly wisdom.

Again, positive living comes down to the choice between earthly wisdom and supernatural wisdom.

> But if you have bitter envy and self-seeking in your hearts, do not boast and lie against the truth. This wisdom does not descend from above, but is earthly, sensual, and demonic. For where envy and self-seeking exist, confusion and every evil thing will be there. (James 3:14-16 [NKJV])

The gift of supernatural wisdom becomes part of an overall spirituality that defines itself by righteous living. This righteous living is the lifestyle of faith that James was advocating for his readers. It is the combination of faith, knowledge, and action that can make a positive impact on the nonfaith world.

> But the wisdom that is from above is first pure, then peaceable, gentle, willing to yield, full of mercy and good fruits, without partiality and without hypocrisy. Now the fruit of righteousness is sown in peace by those who make peace. (3:17-18 [NKJV])

Prayer

Father...may I never accept anything less than your best for my life. May I possess peace. May I bring peace to others. May I base my peace in your gift of wisdom. Lead me in this wisdom, and may I embody this wisdom for others. May I never become haughty or proud. May I never believe that my true power is natural. May I realize that my life in total is a progressive gift. Create in me a meekness that will bring balance and empowered good to all. May this be my legacy.

1. Why do you think that it's important for teachers in the church to be genuine?

_____

_____

_____

_____

_____

_____

2. If a teacher or leader were not genuine in their faith, what are possible negative consequences?

_____

_____

_____

_____

_____

_____

3. How would James describe or characterize a wise person?

_____

_____

_____

_____

_____

_____

4. Define meekness.

_____

_____

_____

_____

_____

_____

_____

5. What is the importance of wisdom being a gift?

_____

_____

_____

_____

_____

_____

6. In John 24:36, Jesus appears to the disciples after his resurrection. His first words to them are, *Peace be with you.*

_____

_____

_____

_____

_____

_____

(a) Why did he say those words at that time?

_____

_____

_____

_____

_____

_____

(b) What does this event tell us about the gift of wisdom?

_____

_____

_____

_____

_____

_____

7. Peace is described as a by-product of supernatural wisdom. Peace is also foundation for the fruit of the Spirit to be made a reality in one's life. List the individual fruits that peace allows for.

_____

_____

_____

_____

_____

8. Read James 3:13-18 and create your own personal prayer.

_____

_____

_____

_____

_____

_____

_____

_____

Say what you will about professional boxing, but you have to admit that a big fight draws a great deal of attention. Ali versus Frazier in Manila was one of the biggest fights in history, both in revenue and worldwide hype. Millions of dollars are routinely involved in these fights. Want a ringside seat for a pugilistic grapple? Better bring a lot of money; they go for the price of an average four-bedroom home.

Of course, it's not just a modern phenomenon. Rome was big on *mano a mano* bouts as well. History tells us that it wasn't uncommon for gladiators to fight to the death in front of huge numbers of Romans screaming with a blood lust—and don't forget those patently one-sided affairs with the lions!

Right or wrong, it seems that it's part of human nature to enjoy a good fight now and then. Of course, it seems to be more popular if the fight is among "other" people. Unfortunately, human nature often finds its way into the church. Both human nature and the inclination for conflict had invaded the early church as is evidenced by this section of James.

> Where do wars and fights come from among you? (4:1a [NKJV])

> But what about the feuds and struggles that exist among you—where do you suppose they come from? (4:1a [Phillips])

> Earthly wisdom causes disorder, but heavenly wisdom leads to peace. (3:15-18 [paraphrase])

James is suggesting that problems related to wisdom are continuing problems. In this case, earthly wisdom is being exercised within the church. The previous chapter(s) detailed the negative end results of utilizing earthly wisdom. In plain terms, it deemed this natural wisdom as demonic. This type of wisdom is born out of the natural state that is inherently carnal and sinful.

As he did in the previous chapter, James begins with a question. Obviously he is conceding the point that the early church was boisterous and contentious. You have to wonder about the root of this inside decay. Was it a problem with former pagans who were having trouble giving up certain tenets of their former religion? Was it a problem with Jewish believers who were still a bit orthodox in their practices and traditions? Both of these possible roots were documented problems within early churches. James doesn't point to a certain group; instead he points to a spiritual problem generic to all. James describes "lusts" and "desires" as root issues in the quarrels and fights of the early fellowship. In the previous chapter, he described earthly wisdom as being self-centered in nature. The same goes for the natural sin condition. Put these two together, and it's hard to imagine conflict not emerging.

Paul also wrote about this issue in his letter to the Corinthian church: *For you are still carnal. For where there are envy, strife, and divisions among you, are you not carnal and behaving like mere men? For when one says, "I am of Paul," and another, "I am of Apollos," are you not carnal?* (1 Corinthians 3:3-4 [NKJV]).

James went on to nail them with the basic truth in verse 2: *You lust and you do not have. You murder and covet and cannot obtain. You fight and war* (4:2 [NKJV]).

An obvious truth to be taken from these verses is that selfishness leads to hedonistic desires. The Greek word for pleasure is the root of the English word hedonism. This state is the antithesis or polar opposite of the selfless devotion to Christ that believers are called to adopt as a result of salvation. If a believer does not move toward Christ in this selfless devotion, they move toward themselves. *All God's children* are moving constantly, either toward God or toward the self. It's as though there are only two directions on this supernatural compass!

These verses point out the human problem of desire. Human nature is self-directed. We, as humans, have innate needs that we are driven to fulfill. It's hard to find fault with this natural occurrence, especially when the needs are basic to life. Desires that are hardly necessary to life, however, cause the most problems. James is describing the progressive pattern of runaway desires that are wholly selfish. Something or someone becomes an object of desire, and the fulfillment of that desire becomes a major focal point.

What happens if this object of desire is actually acquired? "I want it, want it, want it!" Boom, it happens, your wish comes true! It can be great...stupendous...fantastic...or it can be quite disappointing. Something greatly desired is often built up to such a grand degree that it couldn't possibly meet all of our expectations. Either way, the thrill is short-lived. Once it's gone, it's gone. A basic law of satiation comes into play, and in time, it takes much more to satisfy. Fulfillment is increasingly more and more difficult to achieve. Take most drug addictions, for example. At first it takes a small amount less often to bring the desired results. As this relationship proceeds, it takes larger amounts more often to do the trick (and I emphasize the word *trick*). It becomes a never-ending cycle of desire and fulfillment. It's a nasty part of the human condition that requires freedom.

Another point that James makes is that unrequited desire for something can lead to a negative progression of worse sins. The story of David and his intense lust for Bathsheba is an example of a desire that led to more and more sin. The end result of his wanton needs? Murder. The ugliest side of base humanity comes into view when a desire grows out of control. It is the height of selfishness and earthly wisdom.

James paints yet another picture of reality in verse 3: *You ask and do not receive, because you ask amiss, that you may spend it on your pleasures* (4:3 [NKJV]).

Voids are voids, right? We may try to fill the human voids in life with all manner of "stuff," but unless we allow God to "fill" us, it will be a never-ending cycle of failure, frustration, and more sin. If we wish to be filled and also fulfilled, we must simply turn to God and ask. First, we must decide if we desire carnal things or spiritual things. If we choose faith, then we must be sincere and consistent. It cannot be both ways. *Dear God, forgive me for my sins.... Oh boy! I'm forgiven, and I can sin some more!* Asking amiss is a huge problem. God is never capricious, and we can't be either. God is always like-minded, and we must strive to be as well. So asking for something that is patently selfish and self-serving, or even praying for the right things with the wrong motives, is wrong.

Straightforward words fill the rest of this section. First, James states that God is jealous (as does Exodus 20:5). This is not something that most people enjoy. To project human tendencies upon

In This Corner...

God is a bit unnerving. Yet, in this context, the character trait of jealousy is quite positive. Jealousy itself can be construed as either positive or negative depending upon the full range of circumstances. In this case, it's all positive. God simply loves his creation so much that he has expectations and requirements that frame the relationship. He is seeking relational balance, where both sides fulfill obligations. It's a given that God will (has and always will) fulfill his promises. It's the proverbial daily coin flip on mankind's fulfilling the obligations. Again, if we the created do not fulfill our faith and relational obligations toward God, we move away from him. This moving away from God is a natural move back to self, which is a sin and creates sins. Then James deals with the answer and hope for mankind's selfish choices that cause fights, conflicts, chaos, and disorder. *Therefore submit to God. Resist the Devil and he will flee from you* (4:7 [NKJV]).

The problems have been adequately described by James. Fights, quarrels, discontent, selfishness, and the like have caused sin and broken relationships. God is jealous of our devotion and priority. The root cause is clear, and so is the solution. We are called to resist Satan and to submit to God. The power is clear in these words. Submit to God (which includes receiving wisdom), and Satan will hold no power. Seems simple. It is simple, but still responsibility-heavy for believers. Doerksen defines "submit" as "voluntary subordination" (101). Voluntary is the pivotal word in this spiritual equation. Obedience without subordination is common but essentially comes without passion. We obey out of fear or guilt, not out of a love-inspired passion that would count anything less as a major wrong. Passion, therefore, becomes the next pivotal word. Accepting our place with God with a relational passion will make resisting evil much easier. Obedience will spring from a base of selfless love, not fear or tradition or guilt. In short, we give allegiance to God because we really want to.

I once saw a western movie centering on a range war that drove this point home to me in practical reality. One cowboy was being wooed by the "bad guys" to become a traitor and help them steal valuable cattle and land. They enticed him with promises of gold. His response spoke volumes, "I ride for the brand!" His identity was wrapped up in his choice of "sides." His choice came with passion. When confronted with a choice (an attractive one at that), he followed his passion.

The reality of evil is a constant in our lives and, subsequently, in the church. This reality cannot ever be discounted or ignored. To "ride for the brand" will take a great deal of attention, preparation, and commitment on the believer's part. Moo points out the power and scope of the adversary who lives to disrupt the progress of the Kingdom of God:

> While James has earlier stressed the person's own evil tendency as being responsible for sin (1:14), he recognizes here the role of a supra-personal evil being. The word "diabolos" is used in the Septuagint to translate the Hebrew word which gives us the title Satan. The two titles are thus identical in meaning, both suggesting that one of the devil's primary purposes is to separate God and man (147-48).

God gives us the wisdom and power to combat our evil tendencies and to resist a direct onslaught from Satan. He will not force us to live a life of vigilance and duty, however. If he did, there would be no mention of his jealousy. There would also have been no need for the fourth chapter in James. No, it is up to us. It's our call. Fight with Satan (and subsequently not with one another) or give in (which would certainly lead to fights and problems within the church). There is precedence for dealing with Satan that we can draw from and thus commit to a game plan. Jesus went head-to-head with Satan in Matthew 4:1-11. Satan tried every trick he had to move Jesus away from his mission and purpose. He offered him riches, glory, great gain, basic needs fulfilled, and power. Satan learned the hard way that it's hard to pick out presents for someone who really does already have everything! Jesus defeated Satan the same way that we can: spiritual power. "Since Satan has no ultimate power over a Christian, when resisted he can do little but withdraw" (Peace, Coleman, Sloan, Tardif, 47).

James next leads in a process of repentance and reclamation. First, (re)embrace God; then fully repent (make a virtual turn away from a selfish direction), cleansing heart and mind (verse 8). As a person realizes the magnitude of his or her sin condition, he or she should mourn (literally brought to tears). This full actualization of our wrongs against God should lead to two types of tears—first, tears of sorrow, then tears of joy.

In the Beatitudes Matthew records, "Blessed are those who mourn" (5:4), Luke has, "you who weep" (6:21). Mourning is the outward expression of deep grief, indicating an intense hurt that cannot be easily disguised. Weeping is the tearful expression of mourning (Doerksen, 104).

The other type of tears should include joy. Due to God's grace and (agape) love, forgiveness and a new beginning are readily available. Forgiveness is an automatic when repentance is genuine and the heart is contrite. Humble yourselves in the sight of the Lord, and He will lift you up (James 4:10 [NKJV]).

Need a lift?

Prayer

Father...for the wars and quarrels I've created and intensified I am truly sorry. For the times I've allowed Satan to separate me from you I apologize. For the lusts of my heart and for my patterns of selfishness I ask for forgiveness. Thank you for loving me and being jealous of my attention. You deserve more than I give, and I certainly do not deserve what you provide me. Empower me and give me wisdom as you light my path of peace.

1. Have you ever witnessed serious conflict within a local church? What were the issues involved?

_____

_____

_____

_____

_____

_____

2. James was conceding that conflict existed in the early church. What did he attribute these problems to?

_____

_____

_____

_____

_____

_____

3. Describe the stated and implied progressive track involved when a person wants something but cannot obtain it.

_____

_____

_____

_____

_____

_____

4. What are the wrong motives James alluded to in verse 3 regarding prayer?

_____

_____

_____

_____

_____

_____

In This Corner...

5. James stated that wrong motives were the culprit when a person asks of God, yet does not receive. What are examples of wrong motives?

_____

_____

_____

_____

_____

_____

6. Why does James say that friendship with the world is simultaneously hatred toward God?

_____

_____

_____

_____

_____

_____

7. When Scripture speaks of God as being jealous, what do you think it means?

_____

_____

_____

_____

_____

_____

8. Why are believers who go astray told to "mourn, grieve, and wail." Why is this so important?

_____

_____

_____

_____

_____

_____

9. How does a person "humble" oneself before God?

_____

_____

_____

_____

_____

_____

_____

_____

10. Read James 4:1-10 and create your own personal prayer.

_____

_____

_____

_____

_____

_____

_____

9. How does a person "humble" oneself before God?

_____

_____

_____

_____

_____

_____

_____

_____

10. Read James 4:1-10 and create your own personal prayer.

_____

_____

_____

_____

_____

_____

_____

In This Corner...

10 How's the Ol' Future View?

James ends the fourth chapter with a flowing treatise dealing with how some people approach the future. While the possibilities of how to effectively deal with the inevitable future seem endless, James quickly centers on but one—arrogance. James was probably never accused of mincing words or hiding behind them. He simply stated the problem in a direct manner, albeit usually with a bit of a bite. Take the rich, for example; he primarily equated them with evil and ungodliness. Was he prejudiced against the rich? Could it have been that he saw the rich as oppressive and, subsequently, a partner in the rampant persecution at hand? Or was it the fact that the rich of the day were, in fact, far from faith in God and the masters of myopic, natural wisdom?

The answer could most probably be garnered from a combination of all of these possibilities. Either way, James begins this section with a question that presupposes incredulity. The opening, "Come now," is James at his biting, skeptical best. Phillips uses this approach: *Just a moment, now.* Moo calls it "brusque" (154), while MacArthur labels this opening "insistent, brash and indicating disapproval" (231). At the very least, James has an ax to grind with this patently human and myopic approach to the future. He seems to be throwing the gauntlet down and doing so with great confidence.

James is dealing with a pervasive issue of self-dependence. The Hellenistic cities (including Palestine) were still commercial hotbeds at the time of this writing. Money was to be made in a number of trades and assorted businesses. People were transient, and travel was common. People's future views tended to point to the bottom line of profit and socially defined progress. Sadly, it sounds as if the world hasn't changed a great deal in the past nineteen hundred and some odd years.

Verse 13 leads off with the charge against the presumptive arrogance of people with little or no regard to God's activity level in time and history. *Come now, you who say, "Today or tomorrow we will go to such and such a city, spend a year there, buy and sell, and make a profit."*

> The Greek literally reads, "the ones who are saying," indicating people who habitually live without regard for God's will. The underlying Greek verb means to say something based on reason or logic (MacArthur, 231).

To these people it seemed logical or reasonable to chart their own courses and pave their own ways. They seemed to be into charting "long" courses as well. To plan to spend a year in a place denotes well-thought-out advanced planning. To predetermine your probable profit margin over that year's sojourn is self-sufficiency at its zenith. Both of these are not spiritual exercises. James has been forthright about the call to humility, selfless living, and seeking supernatural wisdom. The selfish exercises that he describes in these verses and those he advocated throughout his letter are poles apart in every regard of origin and practice. *Question:* Who is in charge here?

Obviously, in the example he gives, humanity is calling the shots. These people act with zero regard to God's existence. They are exhibiting one of the most ingrained human tendencies, self-directed loyalty. The problem is, both they and we have the power to do this as a lifestyle. If we wish, we can be the masters of our own destinies. Of course, the destiny we control (or think we control) is short-lived and finite. We will only live for a certain number of years and cannot control that aspect of our existence. But long-range plans are an option, as is getting wealthy by planning and preparation. At what price, though? The more we plan from our brain and inherent talent base, the further we move away from God. What a person does (as being described in these verses) is to self-define success and prosperity. A classic cultural view of both would suggest material gain and resulting position and power. The view of James would demand selfless allegiance to God, which includes attention to his attending will. A better way to frame the question would be, "Who does the planning here?"

Sadly, the end result of this human-based planning and scheming is tallied at death. Suppose a person plans and prepares well and works hard. Material gain and obvious prosperity are the rewards. Status and position accompany the successes. But death comes. All things become equal, and chances for a "do over" end. Was success really achieved? Was it win-win or lose-lose?

D. D. Webster makes the point that we err in the following areas if we chart our own courses: *Time* (today or tomorrow), *Purpose* (we will go), *Place* (to this or that city), *Goals* (to carry on business), and *Reward* (make money) (125).

A different view of these could be as follows: *My time; My purpose; My place; My goals; My reward.*

Arrogance, self-sufficiency, and presumption are all sins that are a daily possibility for all people. There seems to be a psychological point of security in having set plans and solid preparations. So is it wrong to plan? The Boy Scout motto is "Be Prepared." Have they led millions of boys astray? Is it wrong to plan for retirement?

The answer to all of these questions would be "no." The "wrong," or sin, would be to approach life as if God either doesn't exist or doesn't care. Presumption is defined in Webster's as "relating to probability." Probability suggests chance. If you kept the word-play alive, you would move to inference and luck. In this direction, we are moving steadily away from God.

Presumption points to the person, as does arrogance. Anything that points to a person automatically points away from God. Therein lie the problem and the solution. Point toward God in all affairs of life and skip the sins of self-sufficiency, arrogance, and presumption. *Instead you ought to say, "If the Lord wills, we shall live and do this or that"* (James 4:15 [NKJV]).

God's plans include us because they are built around us. We must, however, avail ourselves to them. It takes two to form a spiritual team.

James then moves on to another problem of the presumptive mind, boasting. *But now you boast in your arrogance, all such boasting is arrogance* (4:16 [NKJV]). Another way to paraphrase this verse is, "Not only are you arrogant, you even boast about your arrogance!" The Greek word for boasting is related to the idea of a quack. Webster defines quack as "Charlatan or pretender." Picture a traveling medicine man in the Old West selling magic, cure-all elixir from the back of a wagon. A quack promises or promotes something they cannot deliver.

How can someone boast about the future if they can't fully control their own destiny? Without the power to control or direct the full course of events, one is left to "go with the flow of life's events." There is a certain helplessness in knowing that events will unfold before our very eyes and we have little choice but to deal with them. That helplessness can easily be transformed into reliance upon God for all necessary tools to navigate through life.

> Whereas you do not know what will happen tomorrow. For what is your life? It is even a vapor that appears for a little time and then vanishes away. (James 4:14 [NKJV])

There are but two choices for mankind: to assume control of life or relegate the control to God. All of mankind is asked to make this choice once in a decision of salvation, then on a daily basis as the salvation matures. The end result of these choices will most certainly shape and color this life and eternity.

This poem by William Ernest Henley reflects an attitude of those who believe God exists, but who choose to do their own thing.

INVICTUS
Out of the night that covers me,
Black as the pit from pole to pole,
I thank whatever gods may be
For my unconquerable soul.

In the fell clutch of circumstance
I have not winced nor cried aloud.
Under the bludgeonings of chance
My head is bloody, but unbowed.

Beyond this place of wrath and tears
Looms but the Horror of the shade,
And yet the menace of the years
Finds, and shall find me unafraid.
It matters not how strait the gate,
How charged with punishments the scroll, I am the master of my fate:
I am the captain of my soul (MacArthur, 234).

The harshest words should be for those who follow God and acknowledge his supremacy, yet tend to "do their own thing" in regard to plans and courses. This type of person knows right from wrong. They acknowledge the concept (and reality) of God's will. But, and this is a solid but, they choose wrong and forge their own will. Ignorance is no excuse for these believers, nor is it bliss in the long term. It is a show of practical arrogance. This is the ageless argument of James' writing.

It is one thing for a pagan to be arrogant in life's practices; it is quite another for a believer to do so. It is a patent disregard for God's structure and will. *Therefore to him who knows to do good and does not do it, to him it is sin* (James 4:17 [NKJV]).

Obedience is the hallmark of a genuine believer. Arrogance, self-sufficiency, and presumption are the attributes of a person seeking to be the god of their own universe. *He has told you, O man, what is good; and what does the LORD require of you but to do justice, to love kindness, and to walk humbly with your God?* (Micah 6:8 [NKJV])

To be arrogant or not to be arrogant...that is the question! With all apologies to Shakespeare, the question rises with the sun each day. Will we be humble or arrogant? Will we chart our own course, or look to God for direction and blessing? Since we know the difference, the best choice is clear. But will we make the best choice? The answer to that question will have major impact on the entirety of our lives.

Prayer

Father...make your outlook my outlook. Assist me in choosing your will over my hoped-for life. Help me to resist the desire to depend upon my talents, brains, and drive, instead leaning upon your inspired wisdom and direction. May I see tomorrow as opportunity, not as a step in my long-term, self-directed plan. May my life result in humility, not arrogance. May my life be built not on presumption, but on the certainty of your design. And in the end, may my success be measured in the intangibles of spirituality, not the concrete tally of material gain.

1. Planning far in advance could create problems. List and describe a few potential problems that might result from doing so.

_____

_____

_____

_____

_____

_____

2. Is Scripture saying that it is wrong to plan far in advance? Explain your response.

_____

_____

_____

_____

_____

_____

3. How does faith enter into the equation of planning far in advance?

_____

_____

_____

_____

_____

_____

4. List ways that arrogant people are characterized by James.

_____

_____

_____

_____

_____

5. In verse 14 James takes a sobering position on the duration of life. What could we learn from his view?

_____

_____

_____

_____

_____

_____

6. What is the best way for a person to understand God's will for their lives?

_____

_____

_____

_____

_____

_____

7. What does this verse mean to you? *Anyone, then, who knows the good he ought to do and doesn't do it, sins.*

_____

_____

_____

_____

_____

_____

8. Read James 4:13-17 and create your own personal prayer.

_____

_____

_____

_____

_____

Excuse Me, Sir,
Have You Seen My Heart?

James 5:1-8

With a cursory reading of James, one could get the idea that the world of the early church was inhabited by simply the rich and the poor. While this basically was the socioeconomic structure of the day, James was actually inferring in a thinly veiled manner that the world was inhabited by those who faithed God and those who didn't. James is quite direct in his assertion that those who didn't faith God did indeed exercise faith, but it was faith in material possessions. That approach, the faith in material security, seems to be a prime choice of people over history. Here's how Jesus dealt with these two primary choices:

> No servant can serve two masters; for either he will hate the one and love the other, or else he will be devoted to one and despise the other. You cannot serve God and mammon. (Luke 16:13 [NKJV])

> Do not store up for yourselves treasures on earth, where moth and rust destroy, and where thieves break in and steal. But store up for yourselves treasures in heaven, where neither moth nor rust destroys, and where thieves do not break in or steal; for where your treasure is, there your heart will be also. (Matthew 6:19-21 [NKJV])

One doesn't need a chest x-ray to determine the state of one's heart. Whatever one treasures to the greatest degree will determine what controls the heart. And if the heart is controlled, how far behind can the mind be?

Bob Dylan sang, *You gotta serve somebody.* He was right. Think about all of the enormous possibilities that people have to choose from, all of which compete for control of the heart and mind. Advertisers are cutting edge when it comes to providing stimulating commercials and advertisements that go straight to the centers of pleasure and status. If it looks good enough or promises to provide enough pleasure or to make us feel better about ourselves, it will likely be successful.

It's amazing, however, that believers could/would continue to place prime emphasis on material things or personal pursuits that serve the "self." It was a problem then, and it remains a problem today, but why? It's not like one must give up hobbies or sports or making money when God's salvation is accepted. There is no vow of poverty that accompanies salvation, nor are there biblical prohibitions against golf, tennis, or gardening. Salvation does come with accompanying expectations, namely that a person will place their primary focus on God. Remember, God has gone on record as being a "jealous" God. He wants to be where "our heart is" (Matthew 6:21).

With this in mind, it's easy to find the full scope of meaning in James' first words. He begins by wailing away at the oppressive rich who embody the "wine, women, and song" mentality of living for today. These people may have begun with at least partially correct motives, but over time the desire for gain has corrupted them. Over time they have acquired a great deal. They "have," but in the end, what exactly do they have? They have triumphed (in the social/cultural context), but in the end, at what price victory? The final state of riches isn't painted as a pretty picture by James. Utilizing author's paraphrase, the first six verses speak volumes about "riches at all costs."

> "You weep and howl at your miseries." (Verse 1)
> "Your riches are corroded." (Verse 2)
> "You have heaped up treasures, but time's up." (Verse 3)
> "You ripped off people who worked for you." (Verse 4)
> "You sought and bought pleasure and luxury, but how's it all
>   look now?" (Verse 5)
> "You did anything to get rich; how rich do you feel now?"
>   (Verse 6)

They hoarded their wealth...they cheated to acquire it...they killed to get it...they foolishly spent it.

Not hard to tell where the heart was, huh? But James (nor other writers) was in no way saying that wealth in general was or is bad. On the contrary, Proverbs 10:22 reads: *It is the blessing of the LORD that makes rich, and He adds no sorrow to it* (NAS).

Paul in 1 Timothy 6:10 wrote: *The love of money is a root of all sorts of evil* (NAS).

It appears to be a heart thing for sure. Money is fine; just don't love it to spiritual death. Great toys are great; just don't obsess about them. Golf is a fun sport; just don't eat, sleep, and drink it.

Money (and accompanying material things) can have a corrupting power that is easily abused. It is as though a person controls money in the beginning, but the roles are switched quite easily. So money and material things are both trials and temptations (chapter one). They are to be endured, not entertained. They are to be utilized, never focused upon. It's most certainly a heart thing!

Next, James shifts attention to the future hope all believers have in Christ. The first verses majored on the reality of finite hopes and securities. This section centers on the transcendent hope of the Second Coming. Remember that this letter was written to believers who had been dispersed due to religious persecution. This direct persecution brought trials, poverty, loneliness, fears, and concerns. James had already urged endurance through it all, an endurance fueled by hope.

He previously had urged the poverty-stricken to look past the miseries of their present situation and ahead to the glorious future that God has promised. An anchor of that future hope was the return of Jesus Christ. For these troubled, yet strong believers, Jesus couldn't return fast enough. Paul also dealt with this "future hope" in Romans 8:18: *For I consider that the sufferings of this present time are not worthy to be compared with the glory to be revealed to us* (NAS).

Aside from the "future" benefits of Christ's return, another positive of focusing upon the Second Coming is the motivation to live a godly existence. Since no one knows exactly when it will occur, the best bet is to be ever ready. *Everyone who has this hope fixed upon Him purifies himself, just as He is pure* (1 John 3:3 [NAS]).

The obvious idea here is to live a life worthy of Christ's imminent return. *Therefore, beloved, looking to these things, be diligent to be found by him in peace, without spot and blameless* (2 Peter 3:14 [NKJV]).

While we have no clue as to exactly when Christ will return, we do know that it will happen. *Question:* How has the reality of Christ's return made a difference in your day-to-day living? The answer to that question speaks volumes about your focus...and don't forget, it really *is* a heart thing!

Prayer

Father...forgive me of my wanton ways. I apologize for the times I've obsessed about money and other stuff. I am truly sorry for focusing on the bottom line or on the end of the month rather than faithing you with more zeal. For every dollar I've spent out of my own wisdom rather than accepting your wisdom, I repent. Teach me to be patient...establish my heart in your presence...lead me to endure. May I be found worthy of bearing your name.

1. Explain or define faith as you would to a non-Christian.

_____
_____
_____
_____
_____
_____

2. List five things in your life that compete for priority or control of your heart.

_____
_____
_____
_____
_____
_____

3. How would you explain the fallacies and dangers of the "wine, women, and song" mentality of living for today to a non-Christian?

_____
_____
_____
_____
_____
_____

4. In short, describe what James was saying about the rich and their riches in verses 1-6.

_____
_____
_____
_____
_____
_____

5. List five potential dangers of the love of money or material possessions.

_____

_____

_____

_____

_____

_____

6. James consistently dealt with the need for the poor to look to their "future hope." Read Romans 8:18 and describe this "future hope."

_____

_____

_____

_____

_____

7. How does the knowledge that Christ will return again affect your daily life?

_____

_____

_____

_____

_____

8. Read James 5:1-8 and create your own personal prayer.

_____

_____

_____

_____

_____

Bibliography

Cedar, Paul A. *The Communicator's Commentary on James.* Waco TX: Word Books, 1984.

Doerksen, Vernon. *James.* Chicago: Moody Press, 1983.

Jones, Laurie Beth. *Jesus in Blue Jeans.* New York: Hyperion, 1997.

Lahaye, Tim and Bob Phillips. *Anger Is a Choice.* Grand Rapids MI: Zondervan, 1982.

Lenski, R. C. H. *The Interpretation of the Epistle to the Hebrews and the Epistle of James.* Minneapolis: Augsburg, 1966.

MacArthur, John Jr. *The New Testament Commentary, James.* Chicago: Moody Press, 1998.

McGrath, Alister and J.I. Packer. *Manton on James.* Nottingham, England: Crossway Books, 1995.

Moo, Douglas J. *Tyndale New Testament Commentary, James.* Grand Rapids MI: Eerdmans, 1985.

The New Testament in Modern English. Translated by J. B. Phillips. London: Cox & Wyman Ltd., 1959.

Peace, Richard, Lyman Coleman, Andrew Sloan, Cathy Tardif. *James: Walking the Talk.* Littleton CO: Serendipity House, 1998.

Random House Webster's College Dictionary. New York: Random House, 1991.

Stulac, George M. *James.* Downers Grove IL: InterVarsity Press, 1993.

Webster, Douglas D. *Finding Spiritual Direction.* Downers Grove IL: InterVarsity Press, 1991.